Mother's Planning Guide for Secret Keeper GIRL

The Power of True Beauty & Modesty

8 Great Dates For You & Your Daughter

by Dannah Gresh for Moody Publishers and FamilyLife

MOODY PUBLISHERS

CHICAGO

☆

Book Cover and Interior Design: www.DesignbyJulia.com
Some images: © arttoday.com
Photography: Steve Tressler, Mountain View Studios

1 3 5 7 9 10 8 6 4 2

Printed in the United States of America

To my mother, Kay Barker,

who told me the teacup story

and taught me to live it.

Thank you for praying this

verse over my life.

"Look . . . and be utterly

amazed. For I am going to

do something in your days

that you would not believe,

even if you were told."

(Habakkuk 1:5)

Contents

A Big SKG Squeeze to . . .

Moody Publishers and FamilyLife for joining together to conceive and give birth to SKG. What a marriage it has been! I am especially thankful for Greg Thornton, Bill Thrasher, Elsa Mazon, Dave DeWit, and Mark Tobey from Moody and Mark Whitlock, Gregg Stutts, Betty Rogers, and Hugh Duncan from FamilyLife.

Julia Ryan has outdone herself once again with fabulous graphic design. And Cheryl Dunlop, my faithful friend and vigilant editor, didn't let anything get by without being just right! Steve Tressler of Mountain View Studios took most of these wonderful shots amidst a litter of eight- to twelve-year-old girls.

Speaking of photos, aren't the models in this book precious? They're very special ladies from my own hometown, and, in one case, my own home! Thank you to Lexi Gresh, Tatum Stauffer, Alyse Fong, Jessica Fenton, Kelly McGinness, Julienne Baptists, Piakene Nankhuni, and Hannah McCardle. Several of these precious models were guinea pigs to let me try out my ideas. Lexi, Kelly, Julienne, and Piakene were my little small group who learned through tea parties, facials, and trying out the SKG devotions. They were great encouragers.

My special friends Kim Sublett and Janet Mylin helped make the models look just perfect with hair and make-up artistry and showed up in a few of our best shots. Hugs to Rebecca St. James for jumping on board and candidly sharing her beauty secrets and fears.

I am very grateful to Melinda Ohlson, who kept my office running in my mental absence while I wrote this. Thanks, Melinda! I'm back!

The biggest squeeze goes to my main squeeze, Bob. His ideas are the compass that directs me to the end result. His encouragement is the fuel that gets me there. I love you, Zeenie!

Mostly, thanks to Jesus who I long to be with every day.

I am forever in His Great Love.

Dannah

A Mother's Seasons of Emotion

Well, here you are.

A woman.

A mother.

How do you *feel* today?

Beautiful or boring?

Well-groomed or well-worn?

Are your kids ready to name you Nag of the Universe because it's "that time of the month"? Or is your husband ready to name ovulation a national holiday because it's *that* time of the month?

Are you feeling overweight? Or tan and toned?

Are your friendships building you up and giving you courage? Or have they left you raw and lonely?

Is your heart in a good place and filled with strength and confidence? Or are you carrying a wilted spirit?

Me?

My brain is mush today. I can count on these days. Every month. There are three of them. I'm extra tired. I'm thirsty like I just ran a mile. (Believe me. It's been years!) I have a dull headache. To my husband and kids I *am* a dull headache! I feel a little lonely. I'm weepy. And my brain . . . what was I just thinking . . . ah, yes . . . pure mush! (Oh, Holy Spirit, guide these fingers as they type today!)

But catch up with me in a few days. I'll be back on top of the game again. Energetic! Confident! Thinking a mile a minute even if I can't run one if my life depended on it. Enjoying my fabulous family.

Can you identify?

We women certainly are . . . well, I've heard it termed "emotionally wealthy"! I like to think of it as little seasons of emotional change.

Sometimes it's a mini-season like a day or two of a hormonal shower. Sometimes it's like an extra-long winter that just won't warm—brought on by the loss of a family member, the loss of a job, the rebelling of a child or the sickness of a spouse, the death of a dream, or the judgment of a friend.

I had one of those long winters last year. Loneliness. Rejection. Numbness. Tears. A loss of direction.

During that long winter of growth my friend Mary Lee visited.

"What do you sense in me?" I asked, wondering if I was as bad off as I felt.

"A wilted spirit," she empathized.

Tears flowed.

I felt pretty wilted.

She prayed specifically for God to water my soul. Funny thing. He did! The next morning I just happened to read Isaiah 55 as I'd been reading through that particular book of the Bible.

"Come, all you who are thirsty, come to the waters. . . . As the rain and the snow come down from heaven, and do not return to it without watering the earth and making it bud and flourish, so that it yields seed for the sower and bread for the eater, so is my word that goes out from my mouth: It will not return to me empty, but will accomplish what I desire and achieve the purpose for which I sent it. You will go out in joy and be led forth in peace."—(ISAIAH 55:1, 10–12)

The watering began.

Three days later, as I studied the writing of Beth Moore, that precious passage was reintroduced with a freshness from her perspective. "Come, all you who are thirsty, come to the waters."

I came.

The watering continued.

Oh, the fresh outpouring of God's Spirit during those seasons of emotions.

Can you identify? Have you found the fresh outpouring of His Spirit during those short mini-seasons like bad-hair days and PMS? Have you felt it overwhelm you like an ocean during those long winters of emotional pain?

Again and again, have you returned to the Word of God to find that it has the power and authority to arrest those unhealthy emotions and replace them with God's truth about your value . . . your beauty . . . your purpose?

You may have picked up this cute little package with the intent of helping your daughter, but I'm praying that it renews you and me too. That it brings us back to the simplicity of soothing our emotions in Him as we train our sweet girls for the seasons ahead.

Won't you return to Him right now?

Bring the wilted parts of your heart to Jesus and ask Him to water them?

Just stop for a moment and ask the precious Holy Spirit to make you a well-watered place of refreshment before you go any further. After all, how can we bring that refreshment to our daughters if we've not first found it ourselves?

"Come, all you who are thirsty, come to the waters."—(ISAIAH 55:1)

☆ *Your Daughter's Endless Season of Emotions: The Teen Years*

Vitamins and herbs.

Lots of water.

A diet emphasizing whole grains and veggies and avoiding dairy and simple carbs.

The freedom to sleep a little more.

A commitment to bite my tongue.

A husband who promises never to ask, "Is it *that* time of the month!"

These things and a well-marked calendar pretty much get me through PMS!

Hopefully, like me you've learned to identify the patterns of your emotions and have found strategies to regulate them.

But did you have that maturity when you were blindsided by hormones when you were twelve? Do you remember the hopelessness that enveloped you when you woke up with your nose spackled with another outbreak of acne? Did you ever just fling yourself on your bed and lie there for hours wondering if the world would even notice if you were gone? Did you ever completely avoid looking in a mirror altogether because it made you feel so bad? How about the day that your friends didn't include you . . . again? Or the way that you had stomach cramps on the first day of school every single year wondering if you'd know anyone in your classes?

Oh, my sweet new friend, our dear daughters are about to enter into a season of emotion that's been unknown to them. Their little bodies are soon to be barraged with once-foreign chemicals. Their minds will be gripped by thoughts they still can't imagine thinking. The long winter of emotion will seem to last forever. They will have days, weeks, or even months when they feel as if they've been called to climb Mt. Everest in the midst of a blizzard with no sign of a warm fire or cozy tent. The time to arm them with truth to make it through that season is now!

Dennis and Barbara Rainey liken the many perils of the teen years to a field full of bear traps—traps with grim, gray, steel-toothed jaws. They say:

Those traps, what about them? How much of a threat are they? We are convinced that far too many parents are lulled to sleep during the tranquil elementary years. Unaware of the approaching perils of adolescence and of how quickly they arrive. [1]

Our girls are as naive as we once were. And sometimes as mothers we fail to recognize just how many more traps are out there now and how much more quickly our girls find them.

For starters, girls are beginning to menstruate earlier. Most girls begin between the ages of ten and thirteen, but some begin as early as nine. Now, what fourth grader do you think deserves the hassle of pads before recess? Along with the pads you might also see this lovely list of character traits in your daughter:

- unpredictable emotional outbursts
- a quarrelsome spirit
- lack of self-confidence
- loss of interest in hobbies and tasks
- inability to concentrate (otherwise known as mush brain!)
- sensitivity to noise
- irritability, nervousness
- food binges

Of course, the food bingeing for you and me was kind of like, "Hey, pass the chocolate!" followed by giggles. Today, such food binges aren't to be laughed at as they can start a terribly disruptive cycle into bulimia or anorexia. (While bulimia—bingeing and purging—commonly starts during the high school or college years and affects about 4 percent of all young women . . . watch out for anorexia—excessive dieting and denying the body of food. It often targets the *brightest* girls . . . the *highest* achievers . . . in their *early* adolescent years. It only affects about 1 percent of young women, but once it has made itself a home, it's among the most difficult psychiatric disorders to treat and has the highest fatality rate! See www.anred.com for more information.) We cannot be naive to think that our daughters won't fall prey. They are being fed a lie of what a beautiful body looks like. The average model today weighs 23 percent less than the average woman today. When you and I were teens, the average model was only 8 percent thinner than the average woman.[2] A recent Harvard study showed that two-thirds of *underweight* twelve-year-old girls thought they were fat.[3]

Hormones and body-image lies aren't the only traps. Boy craziness hits during the pre-teen years if not the early elementary years. It may not hit your daughter, but it's certain to hit her circle of friends. Some parents passively laugh at this "cute" little trend. Let me let you in on a secret. Being in a dating relationship for six months or longer is a significant risk factor for teen sex. Since a girl's primary sexual organ is really her heart, the longer she stays in a relationship the more she lets her guard down. Can you see how this cute little boy craziness can be a set-up for serial dating that places her heart and body at risk?

Hormones, eating disorders, and physical relationships aren't the only traps. Depression is a greater factor among teens today. The suicide rate among teen girls is rising.

Many of these factors and other high risk activities in our pre-teen and teen young women can be traced to a preoccupation with their body image and sense of beauty. A bad hair day or a broken nail can become an obsession. Some girls will spend more time in front of the mirror than in their school books. Tiny flaws will attempt to rule their mind. We simply must rise up to speak truth to our daughters, women!

And, of course, we can't talk about the truth of their bodies without hitting the subject of fashion. (I'd personally like to hit it with a semi!) Belly rings. Mini-skirts. Bare midriffs. The month I began this project, *USA Today* ran an article on the newest fashion rage . . . exposing your pelvic bone. Photos of Pink, Britney Spears, and Janet Jackson call today's teens to first starve themselves and then expose themselves.

I'm mad!

But I'm also hopeful.

Look at the fabulous women who made an impact on our world *during their own tumultuous season of teen emotions*.

Joan of Arc.

Anne Frank.

Rachel Scott.

Mary, the mother of our Lord Jesus Christ.

And without a doubt each of these was climbing Mt. Everest in a blizzard! I believe with all my heart that the primary reason Satan sets so many traps for our precious teens is that he knows how much power and potential they can unleash on our world.

God clearly says that you and I should not despise our daughters' youth. Instead, we should encourage them to be an example to believers in conduct, in faith, and in purity.

We can stay mad, or we can get smart.

Let's intelligently and lovingly arm our daughters with truth for the season ahead. This edition of *Secret Keeper Girl* focuses on your daughter's image of her body and how she'll chose to present it in the years to come. It will not only help you teach your daughter truth about her beauty and what God thinks about fashion, but it will also teach her the art of soothing her emotions in the precious refreshment of the Spirit of God.

And perhaps a strategically timed batch of fresh, hot brownies!

"Don't let anyone look down on you because you are young, but set an example for the believers in speech, in life, in love, in faith and in purity."—1 TIMOTHY 4:12

NOTES
1. Dennis and Barbara Rainey, *Parenting Today's Adolescent* (Nashville: Nelson, 1998), 5.
2. Becky Freeman, *Mom's Everything Book for Daughters* (Grand Rapids: Zondervan, 2002), 29.
3. Ibid., 30.

Introductory Chapter Three
How to Use Secret Keeper Girl

I know when Lexi falls asleep at night.
Her mouth stops moving.
She's been like that since birth.
Sometimes out of sheer self-preservation, I tune out. That little beauty is on to my game. Every now and then just as I'm about to immerse myself in my imaginary bath of Calgon I hear her little voice bursting through my fantasy.

"Mom, *what* did I just say?" she challenges.

I know I'm not alone here. At some of my events I ask the teen girls what they most want to change about the way their moms communicate. Nearly every time a hand will raise and a freckle-faced, braces-laden beauty will say, "Like, she sometimes isn't very focused when she talks to me. If she could, like, just not wash the dishes or totally stop taking out the trash when I'm talking and, like, well, really, totally look me in the eyes and, like, listen!"

Right about then I start feeling, like, really totally guilty!

One of the greatest factors to reducing high-risk teen behaviors such as early sexual activity, violence, and substance abuse is parent/child connectedness. Translated: "like, well, really, totally looking our kids in the eyes and, like, listening!" My dream for *Secret Keeper Girl* is for it to be a tool that gives you and your daughter focused time to connect about critical issues.

Secret Keeper Girl is really eight great dates for you and your daughter. Each date will be approximately one and a half hours long, excluding your planning and extraneous travel time during the date. Be sure to take a camera along for at least some of the dates so she can have photos for her scrapbook! You may do it weekly or just spread it out and do it as you can schedule it into your life. Just don't let them get too far apart. While each date will have a different topic and activities and even a slightly different order of events, they will all have the same "sections." Your date from start to finish will include the following:

SKG • Prep Talk

The Prep Talk gives you a little challenge of your own and an overview of the date. It's best if you plan to read through this section a minimum of SEVERAL days in advance. That way you can make appointments or reservations or schedule special guests into the date.

 ## SKG • CD • 7–10 Minutes

Just pop the compact disc for the corresponding date into your car's player and you'll get the date rolling as you travel to your destination. I'll be there with you to share a story and get your hearts thinking in the right direction.

SKG • Diary Girl Gab • 15–25 Minutes

This is major girl talk. You and your daughter will have similar pages in your individual books to guide you. These may include reading and discussing Bible verses or completing evaluations or taking inventories. Sometimes SKG Diary Girl Gab comes before the challenge, and sometimes it follows it.

SKG • Challenge • 30–45 Minutes

This is the real fun! The challenge is what you'll do at your special destination. (Think: facials, tea parties, and shopping!) These are either object lessons or simply outright challenge assignments from which you can learn.

Here's an overview of them.

Date Number One:

Your Beauty in God's Eyes

Challenge Activity: A tea party
Key Verse: Isaiah 64:8
Key Thought: A Secret Keeper Girl is God's masterpiece.
Suggested Challenge Setting: A tearoom

Date Number Two:

Real Physical Beauty

Challenge Activity: A facial or manicure
Key Verse: Song of Songs 6:8–9
Key Thought: Real physical beauty is the unique qualities
that only I have.
Suggested Challenge Setting: A full-service spa or the
home of a facial consultant

Date Number Three:

The Source of Beauty

Challenge Activity: A quiet encounter with God
Key Verse: 1 Peter 3:3–4
Key Thought: The source of my beauty is the presence of God.
Suggested Challenge Setting: Any place of solitude, such as a quiet
mountain, a sunset beach, a cabin, or even a candle-lit bubble bath

---

Date Number Four:

The Power of Beauty

Challenge Activity: A study of art
Key Verse: Proverbs 5:18–19
Key Thought: The intoxicating power of beauty is my responsibility.
Suggested Challenge Setting: An art gallery

Date Number Five:
Truth or Bare Fashion

Challenge Activity: Shopping with mom in a vintage store
Key Verse: Philippians 2:14–15
Key Thought: I must express my beauty carefully.
Suggested Challenge Setting: A vintage clothing store

Date Number Six:
The Bod Squad

Challenge Activity: Shopping with friends
Key Verse: Proverbs 13:20
Key Thought: My expression of beauty is
strongly influenced by friends.
Suggested Challenge Setting: A local mall or a favorite
department store
Special Needs: You'll need one to four of your daughter's friends
and their moms for this one. Preferably they'll be also doing
SKG or will at least hold to the same values that SKG teaches.

Date Number Seven:
Internal Fashion

Challenge Activity: A new haircut or special up-do
Key Verse: 1 Corinthians 11:8–10
Key Thought: My beauty is ultimately determined by
what I wear on the inside.
Suggested Challenge Setting: Professional salon

Date Number Eight:
Affirmation of Beauty

Challenge Activity: A dress-up date with
Dad (and Mom!) to affirm her beauty
Key Verse: Psalm 139:13–16
Key Thought: God calls me a princess.
Suggested Challenge Setting: An upscale restaurant
Special Needs: Dad (or a grandpa or big brother, but preferably Dad!)

Budget Crunchers:

If money is a big concern, relax. In the few lessons that may be more expensive, I'll offer you tips on how to do it economically. This option usually requires far more time and planning.

Small Group Alternative:

This needs to be fun, and in the area of modesty/fashion, it's really important to build a positive peer pressure among the girls in your church, school, or community. Date number six requires you to have one to four of your daughter's friends and their mothers participate. It's far more effective if these girls and women have been learning the same things you've been studying during your SKG dates. Therefore, you might encourage these same mother/daughter pairs to do SKG "with" you. You'll still "do" SKG all alone, but you'll have two or three mothers taking their daughters through it at basically the same pace so that you are ready to do date six at the same time. (It might be fun for the moms to meet for lunch now and then to update and encourage one another!)

SKG • CD • 3 Minutes

On your way home, just pop the CD back into the player for a special surprise. Recording artist Rebecca St. James will share some of her own secret moments of struggling with beauty and fashion.

SKG • Driveway Prayer • 3-5 Minutes

You'll wrap up each great beauty date with an intimate prayer in your driveway. Don't skip this vital time of growing closer through the power of God's presence. Your book will give you an idea of what you might pray, but feel free to go in whatever direction God leads you for this time.

**Well, that's pretty much it.
Ready to start planning your first date?**

Your Beauty in God's Eyes

Challenge Activity: A tea party

Key Verse: Isaiah 64:8
Key Thought: A Secret Keeper Girl is God's masterpiece.
Suggested Challenge Setting: A tearoom

SKG Prep Talk

School photos can be unkind.

Just weeks before my sixth
grade photo, I'd emerged from the
beauty salon with my first real hairstyle. After two visits, the stylist had
finally relented and cut my waist-
length sunshine-colored tresses.
I left with shoulder-length "feathers"
to rival Farah Fawcett's. I loved it.

6th grade

7th grade

Before my seventh grade photo, I'd emerged smack dab in the
middle of puberty. My sunshine-blonde, full-bodied hair had become
a dishwater, oil-laden cap. In one year I'd gone from having fantastic
feathers to being an ugly duckling.

And I have it all frozen in time thanks to the school
photographer.

My mother became my lifeline of truth. She never told me that
my hair wasn't darker or that my hair and skin weren't oilier or my
body thicker. She just made it OK with her well-timed and not
overly-focused affirmation. She assured me God was just returning
to His masterpiece to do a little more work.

Prep Talk with God

*Take a moment to pray. Pray that God would help you to
pour precious affirmation out upon your precious daughter.
Lift each part of her beauty and body up to the Lord.
Start at her head and work all the way down to her toes!*

Planning Date Number One:

Value Evaluation Tea Party

Subject: Your beauty and value in God's eyes

Setting Options: A tearoom, special restaurant, or bed & breakfast

Materials You'll Need at Your Destination:

- One fine china tea or demitasse cup for your daughter and one for yourself. *(If you're making reservations somewhere, this is probably going to be supplied, but make sure! Sometimes even fine establishments serve in ceramic mugs. That would ruin the object lesson.)*

- Fine cookies, pastries, chocolates, cheeses, dainty crackers, fruit, etc. *(Again, if you're making a reservation they'll be able to supply this. Avoid "regular" desserts or cookies like cheesecake, brownies, or chocolate chip cookies. Think petit fours!)*

- A bottle of good quality hand lotion

- One common ceramic mug

- One Styrofoam cup

- This book

- Your daughter's SKG diary

I want you to thoroughly pamper your daughter during this date. Find the most exclusive little teahouse or a swank hotel and make reservations for an extravagant tea! When you call for reservations, explain what you are planning so you can ask these questions:

1 "Can you serve the tea in fine china or porcelain?" (Make certain that they can serve you on beautiful porcelain or fine china, not ceramic or bone china. If you can't find a place with the right stuff, either purchase some that can be a gift at the end of the date or borrow some of your great grandma's china. The hotel/restaurant will work with you if they know what you are up to, and if you can come at a less busy time of the day. An afternoon tea would be just perfect!)

2 "Can you serve dainty desserts? What would my options be?"

After you've scheduled your location, read through the rest of the date so that you are prepared to present the object lesson during the challenge.

SKG•CD
7-10 Minutes

Play "Date Number One Value Evaluation" from your SKG compact disc as you drive to your destination.

SKG•Challenge
30-45 Minutes

There are three stages to your challenge.

1 HAND MASSAGE

Upon arrival, let your daughter enjoy the environment, and order if you don't have a predetermined menu. But then your very first act of pampering will be to give her a hand massage. Get down on your knees and lovingly use that fabulously scented hand lotion you brought to give your daughter a great hand massage.

2 TEA PARTY

You may end your massage about the time that the tea arrives or shortly thereafter. Then, just enjoy the yummy food and fellowship together.

3 OBJECT LESSON

Now, it's time for you to make this all have meaning. I've prepared a brief object lesson script on the next page. One quick read through should prepare you.

Where to Go For Tea

Not sure exactly what kind of place you're looking for? OK, let me be specific with a few ideas.

A Special Hotel
In Hershey, PA, the home of Hershey Chocolate, there is a nearly antique but immaculately kept place called the Hershey Hotel. They have a glass-walled restaurant that over-looks their gardens. The desserts are far from ordinary, so you could just order off the menu. A special hotel near you may be just the place.

A Local Bed & Breakfast
Some bed and breakfasts actually specialize in custom lunches and teas to subsidize their overnight income. My husband, Bob, and I once stayed in one in Helena, Arkansas, which had a breakfast so lavish that he got confused about what went with what and poured the gourmet chocolate sauce on his eggs. To find a bed and breakfast near you visit www.bedandbreakfast.com.

A "Chick-Food" Restaurant
A dear friend once took me to a place near Virginia Beach called The Painted Lady. This lavishly painted Victorian gingerbread home featured dainty little finger foods, salads and soups, and a live pianist. There are lots of little restaurants like this that would be just perfect.

You may live in Texas or Canada or Australia, but you get the idea! You're looking for a place to be uniquely pampered. Ask around and make a few phone calls.

Mom: This is really special, isn't it! If you could describe in one word how you feel right now, what would that word be?

Daughter's Response: *(Hopefully she'll say things like "pampered," "special," or "loved.")*

 Mom: What if I just took you to the local diner and got you some tea in this cup? (Bring out the regular ceramic mug.) Would you feel as special?

Daughter's Response: *(Usually a girl will say no.)*

Mom: What if I just stopped at an old diner and got you some tea to go in this cup? (Bring out the Styrofoam cup.) What would you do with this cup when you were finished?

Daughter's Response: *(Usually she will say she'd throw it away.)*

 Mom: But tonight we've been served on fine china and (describe the other special circumstances of your date such as "with dainty pastries and the tables are covered in silk linens and . . ."). These three cups can tell us a lot about our value. Like Dannah (pronounced like "Hannah") said on our tape, you are incredibly valued in God's eyes. That's why He takes so much time to work with you as a potter with the clay. Your value doesn't change . . . ever . . . but the world will only see your value based on how you present yourself. In the eyes of those around us, we're either trashable Styrofoam cups, everyday old ceramic mugs, or the priceless china tea cups in the way that we dress, talk, act, or in the places we are willing to go.

Do you ever see girls presenting themselves as trashable in any of these ways? (The ways that we dress, talk, act, or the places we're willing to go.)

Daughter's Response: *(Could vary. She may name a specific friend or stay with general trends. Be prepared to simply direct the conversation for a few minutes. Let her express her thoughts about what you've just said.)*

Mom: Well, I know I'd rather be a precious piece of china, but sometimes I need reminded of where I'm falling short. So, tonight I'm going to let you evaluate me and I'm going to evaluate you.

Mom Notes

....
....
....
....
....
....
....
....
....
....
....
....
....
....
....
....
....
....
....
....
....
....
....
....
....
....
....
....
....
....
....

SKG • Diary
Girl Gab • 15-25 Minutes

This will be the first time you present your daughter with her SKG Diary. You might want to gift wrap it or put it in a fun bag with a special pen. Give her some time to flip through the pages to see how fun it looks.

The first page of your daughter's diary will be a little welcome from me to her and will challenge her to recall the key thought from the SKG CD. In this section of your book, I have included the same material, but you have all the answers. (Unless the answers are subjective, in which case you still have to think!)

During each Diary Girl Gab time, you'll let your daughter read the little introduction and fill in the blanks for her key thought. Help her if she needs it. These are often tucked pretty deeply into the SKG CD teaching.

Then, ask her to proceed to the main meat of today's Diary Girl Gab. For this date, you'll ask her to fill out her Value Evaluation while you fill out yours on the following page. Give each other about five to ten minutes to do this and then use the rest of your time to discuss the evaluations.

Budget Cruncher

If price is a concern, just get out your best linens and china (borrow them if you need to) and buy some dainty cookies. It would be best to go off-site to a special place. Ask a friend or relative who has a beautiful home or a lovely porch if you can set up there. Or find a babbling brook and set up a table and chairs nearby. Keep service simple so you can just spend time with your daughter.

DIARY

Date
1 Your Beauty in God's Eyes

Welcome to SKG. That stands for Secret Keeper Girl, and I'm hoping you'll want to be one. What is a Secret Keeper Girl? Think hard and you may remember. Can you fill in this blank?

A Secret Keeper Girl is

a masterpiece created by God.

God Himself took time to carefully craft you into being! You must be a masterpiece!

> "We are the clay,
> you are the potter; we are all
> the work of your hand."
> Isaiah 64:8

girl gab!

Value Evaluation

OK, let's take girl talk to a new level. It's called Girl Gab. So, are you a Styrofoam cup, a ceramic mug, or a priceless piece of china in the following areas? Look over the list and then write an "M" in the proper column for yourself as "mom" and a "D" in the column that you think best reflects your daughter's conduct in that area.

	Styrofoam	Ceramic	China
In the way I talk about my dad/husband		M D	
In the way I talk to my mom/daughter		M D	
In the clothes that I wear			
In the clothes I *want* to wear		D	M
In the way I care for and style my hair		D	M
In the way I care for my face each day		D	M
In the way I care for my body and skin		D	M
In the time I spend with God each day		M	D
In the way I treat other people		M D	
In the movies and TV I watch			M D
In the magazines I read			M D
The friends I select tend to be . . .			M D
My friends tend to pull me toward . . .			M D

Now for each area where you selected "Styrofoam" or "Ceramic" for yourself, come up with one specific idea of how you can move toward presenting yourself as a priceless piece of china.

Areas to Improve the Way I Present Myself

Mother's Example: I gave myself a "ceramic" evaluation for the way I talk to you simply because I tend to be busy taking out the trash or doing the dishes at the same time. I need to be more focused when I talk to you, and I will try to slow down and do that this week by having an after-school snack with you to debrief about the day.

Daughter's Example: I gave myself a "Styrofoam" evaluation for the way I've been watching TV. It's not that what I watch is bad, but I'm watching a lot and I know it. I'm going to try to watch only 30 minutes a day and only after my homework is done.

Areas to Improve the Way I Present Myself

1. The way I talk to Dad

2. The way I talk to Danielle

#13 Consistantly spending time
w/ God

4. The way I treat other
people

5.

After you have had time to share, encourage your daughter in the steps she hopes to take. Or maybe she's just really on track. Tell her how proud you are of her.

 SKG • CD • 3 Minutes
Pop your SKG CD in for the ride home. Christian recording artist Rebecca St. James will share her beauty secrets.

SKG • Driveway Prayer • 3-5 Minutes
As you arrive home, spend a few minutes alone in the car praying for each other in such a way that you affirm each other as a masterpiece of God.

Real Physical Beauty

Challenge Activity: A facial or manicure

Key Verse: Song of Songs 6:8–9
Key Thought: Real physical beauty is the
unique qualities that only I have.
Suggested Challenge Setting Options: A full-service spa
or the home of a facial consultant

SKG Prep Talk

Certainly this wasn't happening.

Not yet.

But I could see it with my own eyes.

Physically, I saw a lanky little nine-year-old girl pulling her little body up onto the bathroom counter so she could lean into the mirror. Her eyes scanned the view, studying . . . no, scrutinizing . . . until they sighted a victim—a slightly crooked tooth. She began to press upon that little tooth with her tiny little fingers. Her eyes became slanted, speaking loudly the criticism she felt for this imperfection.

Spiritually, I saw a precious daughter of Christ entering for the first time into a battle she'd face again and again and again.

I wanted to run into that bathroom and set the physical world in order—to tell her we'd fix it and to call the orthodontist for an appointment that very day. Instead, I stood outside that bathroom door and called upon the heavenly hosts to set the spiritual world in order in one little girl's heart.

Prep Talk with God

Won't you take a moment right now to present your daughter to the King of kings. Ask Him to stake a claim at the doorway to her eyes that all she sees when she looks in the mirror would be that which He desires for her to see.

Planning Date Number Two:
Studying My Own Beauty

Subject: Real Physical Beauty
Setting Options: A full-service spa or home of a facial consultant
Materials You'll Need at Your Destination:

- A couple of beauty magazines, such as *Teen Vogue* or *Seventeen* (Optional: See SKG CD)

- The spa or specialist should supply everything you need for the facials

- This book

- Your daughter's SKG diary

Tonight is really about getting in front of the mirror and identifying the unique beauty strengths of both you and your daughter . . . from head to toe. You'll do this by getting her (and yourself) in front of a mirror for a special, pampering facial. Learning the discipline of skin care before problems begin can delay or avoid them altogether.

Select your destination. No matter whom you use, try to spend some time on the phone with the person who will actually be servicing your daughter. Tell her the purpose is twofold:

1. to encourage your daughter in the unique aspects of her beauty
2. to train her to take care of her skin.

Read over the rest of the date ahead of time so you can be prepared or so that you can prepare your salon specialist to go over the areas in the challenge.

SKG • CD • 7-10 Minutes
Play "Date Number Two: Real Physical Beauty" from your SKG compact disc as you drive to your destination.

Note: As an option for this date, you may want to purchase a magazine or two that portrays an unrealistic sense of beauty, such as *Seventeen, YM,* or *Teen Vogue.* It would be a good tool for viewing as you both listen to the CD.

Also, on this page you'll find optional graphic

images to support the CD teaching. I WILL NOT MENTION THAT THESE ARE AVAILABLE IN CASE YOU'D PREFER NOT TO SHARE THEM WITH YOUR DAUGHTER. Why? The photo of Kate Winslet on *GQ* is sexual. Personally, I'd rather show this to my daughter and talk it through, but that is entirely up to you as a mother. Since it is an option to show these images or not, there will not be a cue on the CD for you. You may want to listen in advance to get an idea of when to pull them out, or simply keep them in a pile for your daughter to rifle through as you drive.

Kate Winslet Speaks Out:

The above images of Kate Winslet appeared in *People* magazine the month the February U.K. edition of *GQ* hit the stands. The *GQ* cover image portrays the computerized Winslet. The overlapping image is an unretouched photo of the svelte actress. Winslet was disappointed in the *GQ* photo, and she stated, "I do not look like that. And more importantly, I don't desire to look like that. . . . They've reduced the size of my legs by about a third." CREDIT: *PEOPLE*, 1/27/03

Specific Ideas for Skin Care Date

There are two directions you could go for an effective facial date. Either one will be special.

A Local Day Spa

Look in your Yellow Pages or ask around for advice. Call the spa and explain what you are doing. Some spas only accept clients of a certain age. You'll need to verify that both you and your daughter can be serviced.

A Mary Kay®* Consultant

If you go to www.marykay.com or check your local Yellow Pages, you ought to be able to find a Mary Kay consultant in your area. Mary Kay recently developed a line of cosmetics for girls age twelve and up called "Velocity." It tends to be lighter make-up and lip glosses. If you use a Mary Kay consultant, the facial and advice will be free of charge, but it is only kind to spend a little bit with her on some products. Consider giving your daughter ten to fifteen dollars to buy some lip gloss or skin care products. (Treat yourself to something too!)

*FamilyLife does not endorse Mary Kay products.

SKG • Challenge • 30-45 Minutes
Accomplish the following tasks during your daughter's facial:

A. *Compliment her on specific and unique beauty strengths.*
This is simply a compliment or two such as "You have very creamy, white skin. It reminds me of Snow White!" or "Your eyes are definitely show stoppers. They're so bright and blue I think I could swim in them!"

B. *Teach her how to cleanse her skin carefully.*
If you're working with a professional, you won't need to help with this part. If you're doing it at home, here are some pointers. She should learn to:

1. cleanse her face at least once daily
2. use warm (not hot) water and her hands or a soft washcloth
3. touch the sensitive areas around the eyes very gently
4. avoid touching her face excessively during the rest of the day

C. *Emphasize that make-up is not necessary to enhance her beauty at this age.*
   In the year 2000, the Medical Institute for Sexual Health identified the top five factors that place a teen girl at risk for sexual sin. One of them is "appearing older than she actually is." On the other hand girls who "appeared to be their actual age" tended to be less at risk.[1] How does a girl appear older than she actually is? By the way she wears her hair and presents her face as well as the clothes that she wears. Lip gloss and in some extreme cases corrective base make-up is OK, but overall make-up can wait! Having your professional skin expert say this will carry a lot of weight, and if you buy her some special lip gloss to top the date off, it'll let her know it doesn't mean she can't have fun.

SKG • Girl Gab • 15-25 Minutes
As I've used this curriculum in a small group setting, I'm always surprised to find that girls as young as fourth grade are worried about their weight, height, hair, underdeveloped breasts, overdeveloped breast buds, big feet, large nose, crooked teeth, or freckled skin! They're not too young for a serious talk about body image.

   This date's Girl Gab time allows you to find areas where your daughter may lack confidence and need some extra encouragement concerning her body image. It is vital that this encouragement come from you. Studies show that when mothers criticize their daughters' weight or appearance, it increases the risk of eating disorders.[2]

As your daughter points out a weakness or insecurity, your job is to truthfully state a word of encouragement. Here are some encouraging but truthful responses to criticisms.

"Oh, honey, that crooked tooth is getting straighter and straighter every day as your mouth grows and makes room for it. And I think it's kind of cute!" (I've used that one myself!)

"I didn't realize you felt self-conscious about having breast buds. It's really a very exciting thing. Let's celebrate by going bra hunting this weekend!" (Then, of course, do it!)

"You are right, your skin is becoming a little more sensitive, but maybe that's God's way of keeping you well-grounded. Just think how absolutely perfect you'd be if it wasn't for that one tiny flaw!" (My mom used that one on me more than once!)

Budget Cruncher

The Mary Kay option should alleviate most budget concerns for this date. However, keep in mind that you could always prepare your own spa at home, which might be great fun! Simply show up in bath slippers and house coats, cover the same information as above, and use these yummy recipes.

Body Cleansing Cucumber Water

Lots of spas are beginning to serve cucumber water, as it is an antioxidant for the body. Even if you're having an in-home Mary Kay facial, this drink could be a fun addition to your spa night.

1 seedless cucumber, thinly sliced
1 pitcher of water with ice

Soak the cucumbers in the pitcher of water for a few hours before you serve it. This releases the cucumber juice into the water. Serve in fun glasses with one cucumber slice on top! Makes 4–6 glasses.

Peach Facial

1 medium peach
1 tablespoon of warm honey-cooked oatmeal

Cook the peach until soft and then mash it with a fork. Add warm honey and enough oatmeal to make it a thick consistency. Apply to the skin while it's still warm! Add a few cool cucumber slices to the eye area. Soak in the yummy aroma for ten minutes, then rinse with cool water. Makes enough for 1–2 girls.

(Of course, don't use this if your daughter has allergies to any of the products in it.)

DIARY

Date 2 · Real Physical Beauty

So, can you find God's definition of beauty? Dig deep down under all this world's junk and you'll see it. It's nothing like what we imagined it might be. God's Word says this:

> "Sixty queens there may be, and eighty concubines, and virgins beyond number; but my dove, my perfect one, is unique."
>
> Song of Songs 6:8–9

Can you fill in this blank?
Real physical beauty is

(the set of unique qualities that only I have.)

Real physical beauty is those special things about you that are unlike anyone else. Kind of funny, isn't it? Those are sometimes the things that make us feel most uncomfortable because they're . . . well, different. But God says that's what makes us beautiful. I want you to look at yourself piece by piece today. Can you see that unique beauty?

girl gab!

My Unique Beauty

Complete the sentences below about your daughter. She'll also be completing them about herself. The sentences are to be completed to factually describe that part of your daughter's body and to help her express how she feels. Take about ten minutes to do this. Then, ask your daughter to share her finished sentences with you and spend time affirming her in each area, especially those where she needs encouragement.

Her hair is *(Mom's example: bouncy and the color of your daddy's!)*

....

Her eyes are *(Daughter's example: blue and too small. I wish they were big.)*

....

Her nose is ....

....

Her teeth are...

....

Her face is ....

....

Her complexion is ....

....

Her smile is..

....

Her weight is..

....

Her height is..

....

Her chest is ....

....

Her legs are ....

....

Her hands are...

....

The most unique physical trait about her is ....

....

....

....

OK, let's be real. We all have things about us that make us feel more bashful than beautiful. What's yours?

Size, dry skin, dandruff

....

....

....

....

(Mom, you should share yours as well as listen to hers.)

Guess what? God has got that covered! Second Corinthians 1:4 says, "Praise be to the God of all comfort who comforts us in all our troubles so we can comfort others!"

Some people might try to tell you that braces or zits are no big deal. But they are! Anything that makes you feel bad is a big deal. Just don't forget that God wants to comfort you, and it might just be to help the dozens of other friends around you who feel the exact same way about the exact same thing!

An area where my daughter feels insecure about herself is: *(You'll wait for this one to hear what she says. Record it here so you can bathe it in prayer!)*

....

....

....

SKG • CD • 3 Minutes
Pop your SKG CD in for the ride home. Christian recording artist Rebecca St. James will share her beauty secrets.

SKG • Driveway Prayer • 3-5 Minutes
Spend a few minutes alone in the car praying for each other. Tonight ask the Lord to affirm your daughter in the unique aspect of her beauty and ask Him to pour confidence into the area where she stated she feels insecure.

NOTES
1. Becky Freeman, *Mom's Everything Book for Daughters* (Grand Rapids: Zondervan, 2002), 34.
2. Joshua Mann, M.D., M.P.H., and Joe S. McIlhaney, Jr., M.D., and Curtis C. Stine, M.D., "Building Healthy Futures" (Austin, Tex.: Medical Institute for Sexual Health, 2000), 21.

Date

3

The Source of Beauty

Challenge Activity: A quiet encounter with God

Key Verse: 1 Peter 3:3–4
Key Thought: The source of my beauty is the presence of God.
Suggested Challenge Setting: Any place of solitude,
such as a quiet mountain, a sunset beach, a cabin,
or even a candle-lit bubble bath

SKG Prep Talk

I was twenty-six.

And my life was, well, messy. Mediocre and fruitless at best.

Oh, from the outside it looked pretty neat and clean. Picture perfect really. A cute little house with a yard that had won "Yard of the Month." A husband who was well-known in our little community. A son. A daughter. A nice brick church to call my own.

So, why wasn't I remotely happy? Why was I yearning for something?

Behind the facade my house was cold. My marriage was shallow on its best days and filled with anger on its worst. My kids were confused. My career was exhausting. I was depressed. My church was an unfulfilling social outlet.

Then, one day at the end of my rope I picked up a book that challenged me to spend one hour a day with God. Part of me laughed. How would I squeeze that into my day? Stay up until two in the morning? But I was desperate.

After years and years of a petty fifteen-minute-a-day devotional life, I entered into a daily one-hour scheduled appointment with God. I remember sitting there the first day wondering if the hour would ever end, but after only four weeks of never missing that appointment, I felt myself changing.

My *life* was changing!

It was amazing, but the things they say about Christ actually changing someone . . . I was starting to believe them!

It was happening to me!

That was nearly ten years ago. I'm not quite as much of a stickler about spending one hour a day with God as I was then. Some days I'm engulfed in a much longer time of sweet communion with my Lord. Other days it is shorter. Starting it out as a time commitment was what built the passion and habit and enabled me to begin to truly hear God's voice. I've been changed by this investment of my time.

My life today is a fantastic adventure. My home is warm. My marriage is passionate. My children are directed and happy. My career is more than I could have dreamed of. I am emotionally strong. (Give or take a season here and there that God uses to make me even stronger!) And I'm learning that the church is not a place I go. It is being Christ to those in need around me.

How about you? Is your life what you dreamed of? Or do you long for the purpose and adventure God created you to know? You will only find that place abiding in God's presence, my friend. John 15:5 says, "I am the vine; you are the branches. If a man remains in me and I in him, he will bear much fruit; apart from me you can do nothing."

There's nothing gray about that. You are either spending time with God and bearing supernatural fruit. Or you're doing nothing, all the while spinning frantically like a caged mouse on a wheel.

You need the refreshment of God to feel purpose. To bear fruit in your daughter's life. To be content.

Have you found that place? Are you abiding in Him?

Prep Talk with God

Please pause right now and ask God's Holy Spirit to guide you as you prepare this date. If spending time alone with God has been a struggle for you, confess that and ask Him to fill you with hunger to do it. Pray for your daughter to develop an intimate, ongoing conversation with God.

Planning Date Number Three:
The Absolute Beauty Challenge

Subject: The Source of Beauty

Setting Options: Any place of solitude such as a quiet mountain, a sunset beach, a cabin, or even a candle-lit bubble bath.

Materials You'll Need At Your Destination:

• Depends on the location you select

• This book

• Your daughter's SKG diary

Select your site. If weather permits, do it outside somewhere.

After you've selected your site and collected the items you need, determine if you will need extra time for this date. If you are taking a trail ride or a long mountain hike, you may need to plan for a longer time for this date.

Read through the SKG Challenge and SKG Diary Girl Gab to get yourself prepared to lead your daughter through this neat time with God.

SKG • CD • 7-10 Minutes
Play "Date Number Three: The Source of Beauty" from your SKG compact disc as you drive to your destination.
Note: On the front of your mother's guide is a photo of Lexi and me. Have that ready for your daughter to look at during my "true beauty confession" found on this CD message.

SKG • Diary Girl Gab • 15-25 Minutes
This date is unique. The Challenge will be actually having a quiet communion with God in your special place. You need to do Girl Gab first to set up the challenge. In most cases, you'll do Diary Girl Gab right out in the special place. But if you're doing a snow challenge or a bubble bath, you'll need to do the Girl Gab before you head out to get the foundation for the challenge.

Where To Find Solitude

Here are some great ideas of how to find solitude for this special date.

A Mountain Picnic

If you live near a lovely mountain, hike to an awesome view or find a babbling brook somewhere on that mountain. Enjoy a light lunch or snack as you soak in the smells, sounds, and view. *Items Needed:* Hiking shoes, water bottles, backpack for picnic food and books, blankets to sit on

A Trail Ride

Every girl loves horses. If you and your daughter can ride, find a place to take a private trail ride. The key is that it must be private and you need to be able to stop and tie up the horses for your Diary Girl Gab. *Items Needed:* Long pants, water bottles, backpack for your books, blankets to sit on

A Snow Date

Want to do something really dramatic? There's nothing like the hush of night after a fresh snowfall. If you hit this date in the winter, tell your daughter in advance that your date will be on the next snowfall. When it comes, drop everything to just go sit in a quiet moon-lit field of snow. You'll have to, of course, find a warmer and dryer place during your Diary Girl Gab, but what a beginning! *Items Needed:* Snow pants and coats, a thermos of hot chocolate, flashlights

A Sunrise or Sunset on the Beach

Nothing is more celestial than the beach at sunrise and sunset. When the people have mostly gone and the sand alone is a rhythmic drum for the beating ocean, it's so easy to worship here. *Items Needed:* Bucket to explore and collect things, water bottles or a Thermos of hot chocolate depending on the weather, a blanket to sit on, backpack for your books

A Winter Candle-lit Dessert Getaway

Find a hunter or a friend with a cabin, and gather all the candles you can find and then some. Ask your daughter to wait outside for just a few minutes when you arrive, and set out the candles and light them. Enjoy a gourmet dessert in your special place. *Items Needed:* A cabin, candles, gourmet dessert, water goblets, sparkling grape juice

A Bubble Bath For One

If all else fails and you get stuck at home . . . send all the other family members far away and create a heavenly place right in your own bathroom. Fill the bathtub with bubbles and/or rose petals and the bathroom with candles galore. Set some grapes in a crystal bowl by the bathtub. Then, just let your daughter soak in bubbles while you pray for her in the other room. You can do the Diary Girl Gab after or before she soaks. *Items Needed:* Bubble bath, rose petals, candles, grapes, ice water

SECRET KEEPER GIRL DIARY

Date 3 The Source of Beauty

Where does beauty really come from? As girls we sometimes get stuck thinking it comes from a great haircut or a totally awesome new fingernail polish. Sometimes we think it comes from being surrounded by beautiful friends or being noticed by cute guys. But these are dry streams. You won't find beauty there.

Can you fill in this blank?
The source of my beauty is

(the presence of God.)

. . . .

"Your beauty should not come from outward adornment, such as braided hair and the wearing of gold jewelry and clothes. Instead, it should be that of your inner self, the unfading beauty of a gentle and quiet spirit which is of great worth in God's sight."

1 Peter 3:3-4

girl gab!

The Absolute Beauty Challenge

First Peter 3:3–4 says, "Your beauty . . . should be that of your inner self, the unfading beauty of a gentle and quiet spirit, which is of great worth in God's sight."

What this passage is really challenging is this: "Do you spend more time in front of the mirror making yourself externally beautiful, or do you spend more time developing your inner beauty through quiet communion with God?"

I'd like to ask you to take my **A**bsolute **B**eauty **C**hallenge (A.B.C.). Here's how it works:

 Challenge yourself each day to spend a little more time with God than you spend working on your external self. If your morning beauty routine is thirty minutes, try for forty minutes of time alone with God. Although I don't want you to get caught up in watching the clock, I know that pushing yourself in this area of discipline will change you immensely. Maybe your daughter takes about fifteen minutes to get ready each morning—help her to set a goal of spending fifteen or twenty minutes a day with God. I want you to do this for the next four weeks, for five out of seven days a week. And to make it really fun, put something on the line in the event that you miss a day. For example, you might say that if you miss you'll clean your daughter's hamster cage the next week. If she misses, she might have to clean your shoe closet!

 Agree to the challenge by signing the Absolute Beauty Challenge. When you get home, tape it to your bathroom mirror.

Every day, before you officially start your day, read the verse on the challenge and ask yourself the question, "Today, did I spend more time in God's Word or in front of this mirror?"

Are you ready to dive in? If so, sign the **A**bsolute **B**eauty **C**hallenge on the facing page and rip it out so you can post it in your bathroom. Your daughter can sign the one from her diary and rip that out and post it in either her bedroom or her bathroom!

Absolute Beauty Challenge
(It's as easy as A.B.C.)

"Your beauty should not come from outward adornment,
such as braided hair and the wearing of gold jewelry
and clothes. Instead, it should be that of your inner self,
the unfading beauty of a gentle and quiet spirit
which is of great worth in God's sight."
1 Peter 3:3-4

*"Today, did I spend more time in
God's Word or in front of this mirror?"*

I, ... , will attempt to spend

. . . . .minutes a day in quiet prayer and Bible reading

during the next four weeks. I commit to doing this for

five out of every seven days. If I miss more than two days

in a week, I will . . . . for my daughter.

Part of how I will use this time is to pray for my daughter to
absorb God's truth about her absolute beauty!

Signed: . . . .
Date: . . . .

To make it easier for your daughter, I've included twenty mini-devotions in the back of her diary. You also have these twenty devotionals in the back of your book so you can follow along if you'd like

SKG • Challenge • 30-45 Minutes

After you've completed the Diary Girl Gab, it's time to actually spend some time with God. Give each other just a little space and have your first quiet time then and there. Invite your daughter to turn to the first devotion in the back of her *SKG Diary* and to do it.

SKG • CD • 3 Minutes

Pop your SKG CD in for the ride home. Christian recording artist Rebecca St. James will share her beauty secrets.

SKG • Driveway Prayer • 3-5 Minutes

As you arrive home, spend a few minutes alone in the car praying for each other. Ask the Lord to speak to you powerfully in your devotional time over the course of the next four weeks and to help you maintain your commitment.

....
....
....
....
....
....
....
....
....
....
....
....
....
....
....
....
....

The Power of Beauty

Challenge Activity: A study of art

Key Verse: Proverbs 5:18–19
Key Thought: The intoxicating power of beauty is my responsibility.
Suggested Challenge Setting: An art gallery

SKG Prep Talk

He glances at the curve of your body.
He studies the soft skin of your back.
He reaches for you.
A cascade of chemicals rush through his body like electricity breathing light into a dark stadium.
His mind is washed with adrenaline, blinding his sensibility.
His touch becomes stronger. More demanding.
His body stiffens.
Your body senses his excitement and begins to soften.
The sweet intoxication has begun . . . and you are still fully dressed.

Don't blush! You have a daughter, my friend. At some point in your life you've experienced the power that your body has to intoxicate a man . . . to bring specific and thrilling changes to his. In the context of our marriages, this is a holy act of praise to our Creator as much as an act of passion.

But that cycle of excitement began with a glance. And all too often today's young women are offering young men and older men the chance to study their youthful curves and much of their tender skin. The cycle is commenced. A godly young man will fight it with all he's worth.

But even many of them will fail.

Prep Talk to God

Have you ever taken time to understand the beautiful way God created men to be intoxicated by their wives' bodies? Do you understand how our Christian society is abusing that splendid power? Take time to ask the Lord to reveal to you how important it is to honor this by presenting yourself and your daughter with responsibility.

The Visual Science of Design

Subject: The Power of Beauty
Setting Options: An art gallery
Materials You'll Need at Your Destination:

- Examples of the Gestalt Theory of design (See Girl Gab)
- This book
- Your daughter's SKG diary

This date will begin to establish the foundation upon which we can build the value of modesty. We can't go there without talking about sexuality.

"Hold on there!" you might be saying. "I didn't bargain for that in this study." Well, let me give you a little dose of confidence. There are two reasons we need to go there now, while our daughters are between the ages of eight and twelve. First, for the most part our daughters haven't broken out into full, curvy womanhood just yet. Addressing this now alleviates the confusion your daughter could feel if you wait to talk about modesty after she develops. You don't want her to ever feel as if those beautiful God-given curves are bad. They're not! They're a masterpiece of God. Addressing it now separates the two so she gets the correct message loud and clear. Her body isn't bad, but some clothes are.

The second reason to talk to her about it now is because modesty is, in fact, a vital part of her sexual value system. Don't take my word for it. I bet you've heard of at least a few of these credible leaders:

Josh McDowell states: "Sex education at home must begin at a very young age and continue as the child grows up. . . . If you wait for the 'big talk,' it will probably come too late. By the time you get around to it, your child will probably already know more than you do (or at least he or she will think so)." (Josh McDowell, Why True Love Waits, *2002)*

Tim and Beverly LaHaye say, "By age ten most girls and some boys have learned from their friends about . . . intercourse. . . . Wise parents will share this information briefly, by the eighth or ninth year, to

ensure that their child is accurately informed."
(LaHaye, Raising Sexually Pure Kids, 1998), 84.

Barbara and Dennis Rainey challenge,
"We are going to assume that by the time your
child is eleven or twelve, you have already shared
some of the basic information about sex and
human reproduction. If you have not yet begun
discussing this topic, now is the time." (Dennis
and Barbara Rainey, Parenting Today's Adolescent
(Nashville: Nelson, 1998), 85.

Dr. James Dobson states that "you
should plan to end your formal instructional
program about the time your . . . daughter
enters puberty." (Dobson, Solid Answers,
1997).

We're not going to talk specifically
about sex, but we will allude to the sexual
attraction. After all, isn't that why we're
teaching them to dress modestly?

For your date tonight, you'll select an
art gallery or a museum to visit.

SKG • CD
7-10 Minutes
Play "Date Number Four: The Power of
Beauty" from your SKG compact disc as
you drive to your destination.

SKG • Diary Girl Gab
15-25 Minutes
You'll need to do your SKG Diary Girl
Gab as a foundation for today's tour of
art. Do this either in your car or inside the
art gallery lobby.

Art Gallery Alternatives
The best scenario for
this date is to find an
art gallery, no matter
how small. If you
simply aren't able to
find one, try these
alternatives.

Library
Some libraries
not only have
magnificent books
containing classic art,
but they also have art
within the library.
You'll need to either
go ahead and research
what books you can
look at or plan on
taking the time to
find some great art
in books.

Bookstore
A large bookstore
will have an art
section for you to
browse through. Some
will even have a coffee
bar for you to sit in.
Again, check it out
in advance or leave a
little time to explore
and discover where
the great art photos
are hidden.

SECRET KEEPER GIRL DIARY

Date 4

The Power of Beauty

God created your beauty with a special power. The Bible calls it the power to intoxicate, but it's for just one man . . . your future husband. Each and every day the clothes you choose to wear are a part of saving the deepest secrets of your beauty for just him!

Can you fill in this blank?

The . . . . *(intoxicating)* . . . . power of beauty is

. . . . *(my responsibility)* . . . .

"May your fountain be blessed, and may you rejoice in <u>the</u> wife of your youth. A loving doe, a graceful deer. . . . May you ever be captivated by her love."
Proverbs 5:18–19

girl gab!

A Doodling Lesson
Check out this little graphic.
What do you see? *(Answer: A man)*
Is he happy or sad? *(Answer: Happy)*

Hmmm! I show you a couple of curved lines and a circle and you see a happy little guy! What is up with that? That's the Gestalt Theory. The Gestalt Theory teaches an artist to control a viewer's time by forcing the person to mentally complete a visual image. Because the brain is intrigued by completing the incomplete, it will always pause to finish an unfinished picture.

Check out this trio of circles.
What else do you see?
(Answer: A triangle)

Can you draw a bird using the Gestalt theory?
How about a mountain?

I'm not just telling you this for no reason. It has a lot to do with the power of your beauty. How? Well, what does a guy see when a girl walks by him wearing a tiny little pair of low-rider shorts and a belly shirt? Write your answer below:

(Answer: He sees past the fabric and finishes the picture!
He might naturally imagine seeing her body.)

How about when a girl wears a long, tight skirt with a slit all the way up the sides? *(Answer: The slit invites him to finish the picture in his mind of what is beyond it!)*

Are there any clothes that *you* wear that invite someone to finish the picture? *(Answers: Will vary.)*

What can you do to avoid wearing clothes that invite people to finish the picture of your body? *(Answers: Will vary)*

Now, it's time to tour the art. Your quest is to find and identify the Gestalt Theory in as many places as possible, but I want you to do more than just that. Don't just run through this gallery. Stop at each piece and look it over, savor it, learn from it, and talk about it. Talk to your daughter about what it says about women and beauty. Stand in front of each piece and ask her questions such as the following:

A. What does this say about feminine beauty?

B. Is this a healthy view of women?

C. How does this time period portray women differently from how we portray women today?

D. If you are able to see art from different cultures, how does this society portray women differently from the way ours does today?

Once you've begun to make your way through the art gallery, I want to encourage you to explain in an age-appropriate manner exactly what Proverbs 5:18–19 means when it says a man is "captivated" by a woman's beauty. The actual Hebrew translation would have read "may you be ever intoxicated by her sensuality." There's no need to be terribly specific, and if your daughter is only eight or nine you may CONSIDER skipping this brief discussion. But please only skip it after you've spent some time in prayer asking the Lord if He wants you to do that. I believe that we must begin to give our girls a true understanding of the mantle of responsibility that lies on their shoulders due to their power to intoxicate. I've found that explaining the body's autonomic nervous system (ANS) really helps girls begin to understand the minds of men without robbing them of their innocence. Here's a sample script for you to review.

Mom: Do you remember what Dannah (pronounced like Hannah) said our beauty has the power to do to a man?

Daughter: (Some will remember the word "intoxicate," and others may need help.)

Mom: That's right! Is a person in control when he is intoxicated?

Daughter: (Some will understand what this means, and some will need some help. Explain that it means to be out of control. If they've ever been anesthetized for surgery or dental work, you may use that to give them an idea of how a person might feel out of control, or you can refer to the story on the audio about drunkenness. Be sure to remind them that they are responsible to make good choices, but in these situations, it is simply harder to do so.)

Mom: Well, when a man views a woman's body . . . whether it's her curves or some of her skin . . . he is intoxicated. I want you to really understand it, and I think I have a way that will help you. Do you remember ever being lost in the grocery store or the mall?

Daughter: (Let her share a specific time that she recalls.)

Mom: Well, do you remember how your body responded?

Daughter: (Answers will vary. Maybe she remembers her heart racing or her body sweating or a hot flash that swept over her. Help her along to recall that feeling.)

Mother: Do you remember how long it took for that feeling to come over you?

Daughter: (It was probably immediate!)

Mother: That was your body's autonomic nervous system (ANS) at work. It's the part of your body that is created to respond to what it sees, feels, smells, and senses. You did not choose to have your heart race or your body sweat, but the ANS did this as a signal to you that fear was appropriate. This same system controls the attraction between a man and a woman. For men, there are very clear physical changes that take place in their bodies, just like the changes that took place when you felt lost.

A man isn't meant to experience those physical changes in his body with anyone other than his wife. But here's the difficult thing. Just like you didn't choose to have body changes when you were afraid, a man doesn't necessarily mentally choose to become intoxicated. He is intoxicated by what he sees in the environment. Let me make sure that you understand this is a good thing.

Who created our bodies to have that power?

Daughter: (God)

Mom: Who created men's bodies to respond to that power by being intoxicated?

Daughter: (God)

Mom: So, the response is God's plan, but did you notice that the verse Dannah shared with us said, "Rejoice in THE wife of your youth"? How many wives?

Daughter: One

Mom: So, the man is only supposed to be intoxicated by ONE woman. So how many men do you think God wants you to be intoxicating to?

Daughter: One

Mom: A woman's belly. A young teen's bra strap. A beautiful woman in a really tight shirt. These things can all trigger a young man's "intoxication" response. So, can you see how important it can be to dress in such a way as to honor the way God created men? So, based on this Gestalt Theory, do you think that sometimes the way a girl dresses could intoxicate a man without her realizing it?

Daughter: Yes

Mom: What are some examples of today's popular fashion statements that you think might open up a man's mind to "finish the picture"?

Daughter: She might come up with some things like low-riders, belly shirts, belly rings, mini-skirts, super-short shorts, bikinis, backless shirts, and more.

Mom: There are a lot of things that might do that today, aren't there? That's why I want you to be careful about the way that you dress. It's why I try to be careful. I want to save the deepest secrets of my beauty to intoxicate just your dad (or, if a single mom, my future husband if God would have me to marry sometime). I want you to save the deepest secrets of your beauty to intoxicate just your future husband. Does that make sense to you?

Spend some time answering any questions she may have about this and helping her to find some examples of the Gestalt theory in the art museum, or look for it on billboards on the way home!

 SKG • CD • 3 Minutes
Pop your SKG CD in for the ride home. Christian recording artist Rebecca St. James will share her beauty secrets.

SKG • Driveway Prayer • 3-5 Minutes
As you arrive home, spend a few minutes alone in the car praying for each other. Ask the Lord to help your daughter to understand the power of her beauty and to desire to save the deepest secrets of that beauty for one man . . . her future husband.

Date 5

Truth or Bare Fashion
Challenge Activity: Shopping with Mom

Key Verse: Philippians 2:14–15
Key Thought: I must express my beauty carefully.
Suggested Challenge Setting: A vintage clothing store

SKG Prep Talk

Here I was. Thirty-four. Feeling fourteen.

When I'd purchased this outfit earlier in the day, it seemed perfect. The lime green T-shirt and linen overalls just "felt" like the beach. And the color really made me look tan! I couldn't wait to wear them, so I didn't. It seemed like a good choice. Until I got to this popular Southern California restaurant. Every single woman was dressed to kill.

A brunette walked in wearing tight leather pants and a white spaghetti-strapped tank.

A beach-blonde sauntered in still wearing her dark sunglasses. Her mini-skirt showed off her tan all the way to her slim thighs.

A woman ten years my senior strutted by me looking far sexier than me in her simple tattered white shorts, silky blouse, and high heels.

So, here I was looking at myself in the bathroom mirror of this California hot spot.

I felt like a big green blob!

Prep Talk to God

Ask God to help you to be in touch with how it feels to be dressing differently than everyone else. Intercede for your daughter to have the confidence to do that very thing in her life.

Planning Date Number Five:
Truth or Bare

Subject: The Practical Application of Modesty
Materials You'll Need at Your Destination:

- Money to buy one outfit (optional)
- This book
- Your daughter's SKG diary

It's not easy dressing modestly. And it's a lie to tell your daughter that she'll never feel left out. She may feel less attractive than everyone who dresses in clothes that reveal beauty's precious secrets. And, in fact, in dressing modestly she may turn fewer heads even if she is more lovely. We need to:

A. Tell her it's not only OK but a glory to God to stand out

B. Show her creatively what fashionable modesty looks like

There are many sweet Christian teen girls who say they want to dress modestly but are so infiltrated with the world's billboards and their friends' immodest choices that they compromise. Our daughters need to see modesty in action, and they need some practical ways to test the clothes they choose to see if they are modest. For this date, you'll be having a hilarious look at fashion trends in a vintage clothing store. Then, you'll be evaluating trends based on God's Word.

All you have to do to prepare is find the biggest and best vintage or secondhand store within driving range. Then, read the rest of the date to get it into your mind.

SKG • CD • 7-10 *Minutes*

Play "Date Number Five: Truth or Bare" from your SKG compact disc as you drive to your destination.

SKG • $Challenge$ • 30-45 *Minutes*

For the challenge portion, find as many different "looks" as you can and try them on. You should each try on four full outfits including belts, hats, shoes, and any other crazy thing that might be on hand. The catch is that each outfit has to be a different "look." You might be the polyester queen in a pant suit from the seventies for one outfit. For another, go for the fifties flared skirt and cardigan. (Don't forget the Keds and bobby socks.) This may be easier for you than for your daughter given that polyester suits weren't in style when she was five, so throw out sizes. Size does not matter. Let her float in a ruffled bridesmaid dress from the eighties! The object is simply to have fun and observe how silly fashion trends can be.

If you find something you both like, buy it! Why not! It'll probably be a great deal.

SKG • $Girl$ Gab • 15-25 *Minutes*

After you've left the vintage clothing store, find a fun place to sit to complete the Girl Gab portion of your date.

....
....
....
....
....
....
....
....
....
....
....
....
....
....
....
....

SECRET KEEPER GIRL
DIARY

Truth or Bare Fashion

In the eighties when I was a teen, socks were huge! We had three pair of socks to match each outfit, and we wore them all at the same time! We even had something called leg warmers that were huge, fuzzy socks to wear over our jeans all the way up to our knees! Trends come. Trends go. Does God care about them? Fashion trends are not His biggest concern, but I think He does care. He certainly doesn't want us to just follow the crowd!

Can you fill in the blank?
I must express my beauty

(carefully)

. . . .

God's Word doesn't dis fashion. But it calls us to be careful in the way we express our beauty. If we obey Him, we'll probably stand out a little. That's a good thing.

> "Do everything without complaining or arguing, so that you may become blameless and pure, children of God without fault in a crooked and depraved generation, in which you shine like stars in the universe."
> Philippians 2:14–15

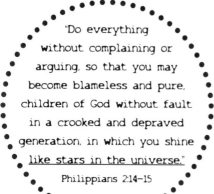

girl gab!

Today's Hot Looks!

OK, let's test all the current fashion trends against God's Word. First, read all the different fashion trends I've listed in the left column. Go ahead and add any that you think I've missed. Include specific things you've had your eye on, like a certain style of shirt or a pair of sneakers.

Now in the column labeled "How I See Them," write down the main characteristics or things people wear when they're trying to get that look. *(Answers will vary, but here are some ideas to get you started. Help your daughter as little or as much as she needs.)*

Today's Hot Looks	How I See Them	Pass, Fail, or Use Caution
The Beach Look	Suit, cover-ups, bikini	Fail. Use caution by keeping your cover-up close-by.
The Prom Look	Gowns, tiaras, gloves	Strapless and low-cut or short dresses still fail. Elegant, long and glamorous is in for an SKG!
Mini-Skirts	Short	Fail
The Cowgirl Look	Leather, boots, hats	Be cautious with the boots.
Grunge	Wrinkled shirts, big shoes	Fail. Doesn't say joyful!
Goth	Black, heavy clothes	Fail. Definitely not joyful!
Preppie	Rugbys, sneaks, capris	Pass
Punk	Neck ties, zippers, suspenders	Caution with zippers.
Athletic	Sweats, T's, wrist bands	Pass
The 50's Look	Big skirts, blazers, tennis	Pass
Designer Labels	Anything that says money	Caution
Belly Ring		Fail. Dad says no.
Tattoo		Fail. Graffiti on God's temple?

Now you can decide if these looks "Pass," "Fail," or deserve "Caution" based on a few Bible verses I think help us evaluate fashion. (Some of these will be familiar to you!)

Is this look feminine?

"A woman must not wear men's clothing, nor a man wear women's clothing, for the LORD your God detests anyone who does this."
—Deuteronomy 22:5

God wants you to look like a girl . . . not a guy. That doesn't mean you can't wear pants. It just means you shouldn't wear pants that are cut for men or anything else that is considered manly in our society. Are there any things above that you feel God wouldn't want you to wear because they don't let you look like a girl?

Does this look hide my "intoxicating" secrets?

"Rejoice in the wife of your youth. A loving doe, a graceful deer. . . . May you ever be captivated by her love."
—Proverbs 5:18–19

God wants you to save the deepest secrets of your beauty . . . your breasts, your belly skin, your thighs, and your bottom . . . for just one man. Does this trend make you look fabulous without drawing attention to these parts of your body?

Is this look joyful?

"I also want women to dress modestly, with decency . . . with good deeds, appropriate for women who profess to worship God."
—1 Timothy 2:9–10

God wants you to look like a girl who worships Him. Since worshipping Him fills us with joy, we need to make sure that we don't clothe ourselves in dark and dreary attire. Are there any looks above that you should avoid for that reason?

Is it affordable?

"Your beauty should not come from outward adornment, such as braided hair and the wearing of gold jewelry and fine clothes. Instead, it should be that of your inner self, the unfading beauty of a gentle and quiet spirit, which is of great worth in God's sight."—1 Peter 3:3–4

God doesn't want you to be consumed with how much you spent on an outfit or whether it's a certain brand. It doesn't mean we can't have a certain brand if it's comfortable and affordable, but we can't whine for things we can't afford. Are there any things above that need to be disqualified for this reason?

Does it honor my parents?

"Honor your father and your mother, so that you may live long in the land."—Exodus 20:12

A Secret Keeper Girl can't wear anything her parents don't want her to wear, and she has to obey their preferences with honor. So, do you need to cross anything off for this reason?

Do I really like it, or do I just think my friends will like it?

"Am I now trying to win the approval of men, or of God? . . . If I were still trying to please men, I would not be a servant of Christ."
—Galatians 1:10

It's OK to want something because you think it's neat, but watch out when you start buying things just because your friends have them.

 SKG • CD • 3 Minutes
Pop your SKG CD in for the ride home. Christian recording artist Rebecca St. James will share her beauty secrets.

SKG • Driveway Prayer • 3-5 Minutes
Take time to pray about your hearts . . . both of you. Is there anywhere that you've compromised in the kinds of clothes you wear? Ask the Lord to give your daughter a willing heart to stand out like a star in the universe!

6

The Bod Squad

Challenge Activity: Shopping with friends

Key Verse: Proverbs 13:20
Key Thought: My expression of beauty is
strongly influenced by friends.
Suggested Challenge Setting: A local mall or a
favorite department store
Special Needs: You'll need one to four of your daughter's
friends and their moms for this date. Preferably they'll be
also doing SKG or will at least hold to the same
values as SKG teaches.

SKG Prep Talk

You like Ann Taylor Loft. She likes Limited Too.
You think "comfort." She thinks "cool."
You wear Keds. She wears Skeechers.

As much as we'd like to remain the sole influencers in our
daughters' lives, that just isn't going to happen . . . especially in
this area of fashion. In a survey conducted for *World* magazine,
peer pressure was named by female college students as a primary
reason they chose the clothes they wear. Our daughters care about
what their friends think. The best thing you and I can do is to
guide them to select friends whose parents are establishing the
same values that we're working toward.

Prep Talk Prayer

*Pray as you prepare this date that your daughter and her
friends would choose to influence each other positively in all
areas of their lives. Pray for her closest friends by name.*

The Bod Squad

Subject: Peer Pressure
Setting Options: A mall or a department store
Materials You'll Need at Your Destination:

- Cash in the amount of $20–100
- Photocopies of the Truth or Bare fashion tests for
  all the moms (pages 66-67)
- Photocopies of the SKG Girl Gab Diary for the daughters
  (pages 65-67)
- This book
- Your daughter's SKG diary

Your daughter and a few of her friends will be learning through the SKG Truth or Bare Fashion Tests. These tests help her to creatively determine if an outfit is modest or not.

Determine who you'll be shopping with. If you know of other mothers who are doing SKG with their daughters, you've already got your shopping buddies. If not, you need to begin your planning by selecting one or two of your daughter's friends who seem to dress in the way that you like your daughter to dress. Contact their mothers and explain what you are doing and get the mothers a copy of the Truth or Bare fashion tests to look at ahead of time.

Determine how much the girls will have to spend. Get your brains together to decide how much money you want to invest in the night. I suggest no less than $20 or they won't have enough to buy anything significant, and no more than $100 or the challenge will take too long. Each mother needs to feel comfortable with what you decide, and each girl needs to have the same amount.

Select a mall or department store that your daughters love. Here's my warning: Be prepared to bomb at some stores. When we shop using these tests, we sometimes have to completely redirect ourselves, especially during the summer months.

Select a meeting place and a time. You'll want to listen to the CD together, so if you all fit into one vehicle, that'd be great!

SKG • CD • 7-10 Minutes
Play "Date Number Six: The Bod Squad" from your SKG compact disc as you drive to your destination.

SKG Girl Gab • 15-25 Minutes
You'll do Girl Gab as a group, so make copies for the other girls who don't have diaries. As you arrive at the SKG Truth or Bare Fashion Tests, ask the girls to try them. If any of them has on an outfit that fails, don't back off the validity of the test, but be kind as you speak the truth in love. Suggest a solution. For example, "Wow. Jennifer, it can be shocking to find that a shirt you never even thought about might be a little low-cut. But you have great taste, and I really like that shirt. Don't get rid of it. Try to find a cool T-shirt to put under it."

SECRET KEEPER GIRL DIARY

6 The Bod Squad

Well, here you are with your special friends, otherwise known as The Bod Squad! (Hi, friends!) I want you to offer each other positive peer pressure. Remember, peer pressure is when your friends or acquaintances influence you to do what is right or what is wrong. Do you remember what I said about peer pressure and fashion on the CD?

My . . . . of beauty is . . . .
     (expression)
   (strongly influenced by my friends)
. . . .

> "He who walks with
> the wise grows wise."
> Proverbs 13:20

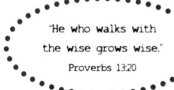

OK, I'd like to update that verse for today's SKG! "She who shops with wise friends will wear great fashion!"

girl gab!

Truth or Bare Fashion Tests!

Before we set you loose to shop, I have a few modesty tests every single outfit has to pass. I like to call them the SKG Truth or Bare Fashion Tests. Review each test and take them as a group.

Note to Moms: Most of these tests aren't relevant to the majority of eight- to twelve-year-olds, so you may be wondering what the point is. Just as we prepare our daughters ahead of time for menstruation, we must prepare them ahead of time for how to handle breast development and curves. Even if some of her outfits are OK now, when do you tell her she can't wear them anymore? When she's feeling totally awkward because her breasts are just budding, or when she's fully round and has been intoxicating many young boys? I think it's better to prepare her now, in a fun setting with friends, and to let her see her developing womanhood as a joyous thing and not a nuisance that "limits" the fun things she can wear. And notice we're also giving her the freedom to hold you accountable, so she is less likely to feel that this is an unfair burden you're placing on her.

Test: "Raise & Praise"
Target Question: Am I showing too much belly?
Action: Stand straight up and pretend you are going for it in worship, and extend your arms in the air to God. Is this exposing a lot of belly? Bellies are very intoxicating, and we need to save that for our husband! **Remedy:** Go to the guys' department and buy a simple ribbed T-shirt* to wear under your funky short T's or with your trendy low-riders. Layers are a great solution to belly shirts.

Test: "Grandpa's Mirror"
Target Question: How short is too short?
Action: Get in front of a full-length mirror. If you are in shorts, sit Indian style. If you are in a skirt, sit in a chair with your legs crossed. Now, what do you see in that mirror? OK, pretend it is your Grandpa! If you see undies, or lots of thigh, your shorts or skirt is too short.
Remedy: Buy longer shorts and skirts!

Usually, your best source for a tank or T-shirt long enough for this effect is the men's department.

Test: "I See London, I See France"

Target Question: Can you see my underpants?
Action: Bend over and touch your knees.
Have a friend look right at your bottom.
Can she see the outline of your underpants or the seams in them? How about
the color of them? Can she see your
actual underwear because your pants are
so low that you're risking pulling a
"plumber" exposure? If so, you bomb on
this test. **Remedy:** Wear white panties
with white clothes. If your pants are so
tight that you can see the outline of your
panties, try buying one size larger.

Test: Spring Valley

Target Question: "Is my shirt too tight?"
Action: The girls are probably not quite ready for
this test, so we'll let the moms take it. You might
start by acknowledging that "we are girls and
women and we'll all be getting or already have
breasts!" (The girls will giggle something silly!)
Have the moms place the tips of their fingers
together and press into their shirts right in the
"valley" between the breasts. Count to three and
have them take their fingers away. If their shirts
spring back like a small trampoline, they are too
tight. Explain to the girls that even though this might not be a
problem for them just yet, it won't be long until they need to be
careful about wearing shirts that are too tight. **Remedy:** Don't
buy clothes based on size. Buy them based on fit.
Usually, you have to go a few sizes larger these
days to have a modest fit.

Test: Over & Out

Target Question: "Is my shirt too low?"
Action: Lean forward a little bit. Can you see too
much chest skin or future cleavage? If so, your
shirt is too low. **Remedy:** Today's fashions thrive
on low shirts. Layering them is often the only
remedy. Throw a little T-shirt under a rugby and
you have a great look.

Is My Swimsuit Modest?

Oh, girlfriend! That is a hard question. I would say that your swimsuit needs to pass nearly all of these tests. Can you raise and praise without showing off your belly? Can you bend over without showing off cleavage? Can you sit Indian style and look in a mirror without your suit gapping at the crotch? And still . . . swimsuits aren't high on the modesty scale unless you're in the water! So, when you jump out don't flaunt your body, cover up with one of the cute little cover ups available today or a simple pair of shorts and a T-shirt!

SKG • Challenge • 30-45 Minutes
After you have completed Girl Gab somewhere, go over these simple challenge rules before you set the girls loose.

A. Shop as a group, allowing the girls' opinions to encourage and direct each other for what they think looks cool and is trendy.

B. Everything they buy has to pass all of the "Truth or Bare" Fashion tests learned on this date and the last date. Mothers will act as a panel of judges!

Present them with their cash and try to keep up!
Be prepared to say no to any outfits that do not pass our tests. Also, be prepared to pep them up and redirect them if they get discouraged. This date is not about saying "no" to immodesty. It's about saying "yes" to cool, godly clothes and creating positive peer pressure!

 ## SKG • CD • 3 Minutes
Pop your SKG CD in for the ride home. Christian recording artist Rebecca St. James will share her beauty secrets.

SKG • Driveway Prayer • 3-5 Minutes
Before you split up, ask all the girls to pray in their driveways with their moms tonight. Pray for each girl and ask that in the years ahead, these girls would be a positive influence on one another in every way.

Date

7

Internal Fashion

Challenge Activity: A new hair style or up-do

Key Verse: 1 Corinthians 11:8–10
Key Thought: My beauty is ultimately determined by
what I wear on the inside.
Suggested Challenge Setting: A hair salon

SKG Prep Talk

I'd admired her from a distance for years. I'd never spent much
time around her. Just ran into her at church, Bible school, or the
grocery store. She had the most adorable dimples and perky blue eyes.

Then one day I showed up at the pool, and there she was.

"Get away," she snarled at her little son. Profanity followed as
she grumbled about how he'd gotten her book wet.

I was shocked. Surely I'd just caught her on a bad day.

A few weeks later, there she was again sunning by the pool and
ignoring her kids. I watched when she and her friend began to
gather the kids for lunch. One straggler found the water much too
tempting and stayed in the pool giggling.

She stomped over to the edge of the pool and began to bellow
expletives at her poor little son. He didn't seem shocked. It looked
like Mom's ranting and cursing was just par for the course.

The aura of beauty began to fade.

I can't even remember what it looked like.

We all know people who appear beautiful until we begin to see
inside of them. Then the beauty quickly fades. In the same respect
some people seem to grow more and more beautiful as we see deeper
into their hearts.

Which are you?

Which is your daughter becoming?

Prep Talk to God

*Ask the Lord to help you focus on adorning your daughter's
heart with more energy than you use to fill her closet and
drawers.*

Planning Date Number Seven:
Internal Beauty

Subject: Showing your beauty through submission
Setting Options: A Hair Salon
Materials You'll Need at Your Destination:

- The salon or specialist should supply everything you need
- This book
- Your daughter's SKG diary

This date is about teaching your daughter that God has "garments" for us to wear that give us internal beauty. We'll do this by focusing on hair, since both the Old and New Testament have encouragements for women to allow their hair to be an expression of the internal garment of submission.[1] You'll have a great time at a hair salon where your daughter can learn more about how to care for her hair and can be treated to a new cut or up-do.

Select your destination. Find a hair salon that's cool and fun to go to. Spend some time on the phone explaining to the stylist that this is a special date for you and your daughter and explain that you'd like to:

A. Encourage your daughter by sharing what's beautiful about her hair

B. Train her to take care of her hair

Read over the SKG Challenge so you can be prepared or so that you can prepare your salon specialist to go over areas suggested in the challenge.

SKG • CD • 7-10 Minutes
Play "Date Number Seven: Internal Fashion" from your SKG compact disc as you drive to your destination.

SKG • Challenge • 30-45 Minutes
Prepare yourself, your salon stylist, or whomever is leading the challenge portion to accomplish the following tasks during your daughter's haircut/style or up-do.

1 Teach her basic hair care. At this age, many of our daughters think a fun hairstyle is cool if they are in the mood, but most of the time when the brush comes out, they grumble! So empower her to be the one to take care of her hair. Here are the basic guidelines:

• Shampoo whenever your hair starts to look stringy or feel oily. That's usually several times a week by the time a girl is eight to twelve. For active girls and girls with oily hair, it may be daily.

• Use a pH-balanced shampoo and squirt about the size of a quarter into your hand. Work it through your hair by massaging with your fingertips, not by scratching with your fingernails.

• Rinse thoroughly until there's nothing at all left. If you have shampoo left in your hair, it'll just get dirtier faster, and you'll be doing it again very soon!

• Brush your hair at least twice daily . . . when you wake up and before you go to sleep. It's a good idea to give it a fresh brushing after you swim or play sports or if you're going to be doing something special like going to a friend's house for a while.

2 Discuss a fun new haircut or a special braid or up-do and let the stylist do her work!

After your daughter has been made to look and feel lovely, it's time to find a place to be alone with her. Most likely, you'll need to drive somewhere to be alone with her. Play a favorite CD of hers on the way. Or you may begin the conversation time while you drive.

This Girl Gab hits some heavy teaching on submission, but I believe our girls are ready for it. After you've completed the Submission Scale quiz, take time to talk about what you can both specifically do to demonstrate a submissive spirit.

Budget Cruncher

The purpose of this night is to focus on your daughter's hair. If taking her to a salon is entirely too expensive, first ask around to see if you can find someone at church who is either a stylist or just has a reputation for great French braids or other hairstyles and would be willing to invite you over for your special time of encouragement. If that doesn't work, try borrowing a book of special braids or hair wraps at the library and learning something special you can do to surprise your daughter.

....
....
....
....
....
....
....
....
....
....
....
....
....
....
....
....
....
....
....

Date

7 ‍Internal Fashion

Ever meet a girl who just looked so cool but then she turned out to be a snob? Notice how her beauty fades? Of course, maybe you've met a girl who at first glance doesn't seem that beautiful, but the more you are around her the more fabulous she looks to you. That's internal beauty you're seeing. An SKG isn't complete without fashion for her heart.

Finish this sentence.
My beauty is ultimately determined

(by what I wear on the inside.)
. . . .

One of the kinds of "garments" God wants us to wear is submission.

"For man did
not come from woman,
but woman from man;
neither was man created
for woman, but woman for
man. For this reason,
and because of the angels,
the woman ought to have
a sign of authority on
her head."

1 Corinthians 11:8–10

Women in Bible days were so committed to the internal fashion of submission that they wore their hair a certain way as an external reminder for themselves and everyone else around them. Wow!

girl gab!

Fashion For My Heart

Clothes aren't all that we wear. God invites us to "wear" things on the inside too. Check out these verses and discover some of the hottest fashions for the heart. **Underline the things we're called to "wear."**

"[A woman of God] is clothed with <u>strength</u> and <u>dignity</u>. . ."
--Proverbs 31:25

"Put on the full armor of God. . . . Stand firm then, with the belt of <u>truth</u> buckled around your waist, with the breastplate of <u>righteousness</u> in place, and with your feet fitted with the readiness that comes from the gospel of <u>peace.</u> In addition to all this, take up the shield of <u>faith</u>, with which you can extinguish all the flaming arrows of the evil one. Take the helmet of <u>salvation</u> and the sword of the Spirit, which is the word of God."--Ephesians 6:13-17

"I also want women to dress modestly, with decency . . . with <u>good deeds,</u> appropriate for women who profess to worship God."
--1 Timothy 2:9-10

"Your beauty should not come from outward adornment . . . [but from] a <u>gentle and quiet spirit</u> . . . " —1 Peter 3:3-4

The things you've underlined are all vital parts of a SKG's wardrobe. But I think the most vital internal garment for an SKG is submission. Submission is allowing someone else to lead you. Submitting doesn't require you to mindlessly follow a bad example. Submission invites you to sometimes let a good friend get to play the game she wants to play even if you'd rather not. Submission requires you to quietly honor your parents, teachers, and other authorities with obedience. What a privilege! (What a tough task!) So, how do you know if you're wearing that? I mean, it's not like you can see it. Let's see if you've got submission hanging in your internal power wardrobe.

Submission Scale Quiz

Circle the statement that most sounds like you.

1 When the kids I'm hangin' with decide they want to do something I don't want to do I:
  a. yell and grumble and run home stomping all the way
  b. keep talking until I convince everyone to do what I want to do
  c. it's hard, but I try to listen to everyone's feelings and help us work it out
  d. do what my friends prefer; after all, everyone deserves a turn to lead

2 When the teacher gives me homework, I usually
  a. refuse to do it
  b. do it, but the whole time I think it's dumb because I already know it all
  c. wish I didn't have to, but I don't want to disappoint my teacher
  d. do it without thinking too much; after all, she's the teacher!

3 When my parents ask me to do something I
  a. throw a royal fit and ask to be paid
  b. grumble and do it half right
  c. feel sad because I'm not getting to do what I want, but I get it done
  d. do it with all my heart because I want to please my parents

4 When one of my siblings wants the same video game or toy that I want I
  a. tease him or her the whole time as I play with the toy
  b. tell him what I think he should be doing
  c. ask if I can have it first and let the other person wait for his or her turn
  d. let the other person go first as I find something else to do

5 When I think someone has made a mistake I
  a. want to be the first to correct the person as loudly as possible
  b. try to take over because I can do it better
  c. watch for a good time to bring it up quietly
  d. wait for adults or others in authority to make things right

6 I go to church because
  a. my parents make me, but I wouldn't if I could help it
  b. I have to, but I never really learn anything
  c. I have good friends there
  d. I want to be what God wants me to be, and church is a great place to learn

So, how'd ya do? Count up all your a's, b's, c's and d's.
Write the totals below.

_____A _____B _____C _____D

Which letter did you have the most of? Circle that letter below
to find out how you're doing.

Submissive Servant
Wow! I wish I could score this high. Keep up the great
work. Just don't let it go to your head.

Sensitive Socialite
Good eye, girlfriend. You recognize your own desires, but
you're trying so hard to put others ahead of yourself and
you often succeed.

Boisterous Boss
Try harder! You probably have a lot of leadership
potential, but God can't use that until you learn some
gentleness. Work on controlling your tongue.

Raging Rebel
Uh oh! Watch out! You're wearing the wrong stuff, girl.
You need to work on controlling your tongue and your
emotions.

𝒮𝒦𝒢 • 𝒞𝒟 • 3 Minutes
Pop your SKG CD in for the ride home. Christian recording
artist Rebecca St. James will share her beauty secrets.

𝒮𝒦𝒢 • Driveway Prayer • 3-5 Minutes
As you arrive home, ask the Lord to give you both a submissive
spirit, especially in the home. If you need to, confess to the Lord
that this has been an area of sin in your life. Give your daughter
that same chance.

NOTE
1. Some New Testament passages that address hair include 1 Corinthians 11:14–15; 1 Timothy
2:9; 1 Peter 3:3. Old Testament passages mainly deal with the Nazarite vow, which included not
cutting or shaving one's hair and was believed to be an outward symbol of one's humility and
willingness to be used by God. Just prior to coming into the tabernacle, the Nazarite was permit-
ted to shave ceremoniously. Such passages include Leviticus 14:8–9; Numbers 6:5; Judges
16:17–22.

Affirmation of Beauty

*Challenge Activity: A dress-up date with Dad
(and Mom!) to affirm her beauty*

Key Verse: Psalm 139:13–16
Key Thought: God calls me a princess.
Suggested Challenge Setting: An upscale restaurant
Special Needs: Dad (or a grandpa or big brother, but preferably dad!)

SKG Prep Talk

It was Lexi's fifth birthday.

My mother and I sat at the kitchen table sipping tea and giggling about the day's events when Bob walked in. I glanced at my watch. He was awfully late.

He looked like the cat that had just eaten a mouse . . . only this mouse must've been quite a catch. He beamed as he walked over to Lexi and presented her with something.

He had all of our attention now.

Her awkward fingers lifted the lid from a tiny heart-shaped pewter box and grasped the shiny gold bracelet laden with blue gems.

"Read the box," Bob encouraged, looking at me. I reached for the box and read the inscription.

For Lexi from Daddy, December 28, 1998, "Something Blue"

Tears fell down my cheeks as I shared it with my mother. Our hearts knew the significance of this precious gift, even if Lexi's bright blue eyes were simply curious and excited.

Bob intends to give Lexi a special gift every fifth birthday until she's received a gift that represents each phrase of the old bride's poem, "Something old, Something new, Something borrowed, Something blue!"

We laugh and say that it's our way of bribing her because she won't be ready for marriage until she's at least twenty, but it's a special love connection between Lexi and her daddy. It's an affirmation of her value and his dreams for her.

Prep Talk with God

Ask the Lord to move in the relationship between your daughter and her father. Ask Him to overcome every obstacle and to create a special newness in their relationship through this date.

Planning Date Number Eight:
Affirmation of Beauty

Subject: A dress-up date with Dad to affirm her beauty
Setting: A posh restaurant
Special Needs: Dad (or a grandpa or big brother, but preferably dad!)
Materials You'll Need at Your Destination:

- Reservations at an up-scale restaurant
- A small, special box
- This book
- Your daughter's SKG diary
- A special gift for your daughter (optional)

I want to bring your daughter's dad into the picture to affirm her beauty. Social surveys demonstrate that girls who have no connectedness with their fathers tend to be more likely to act out in high-risk behaviors as teens. On the other hand, girls who have a close relationship with their dad are more likely to live a life of purity, avoid substance abuse, and be generally well-adjusted as teens. I always encourage dads of teen girls to make sure that their daughter gets at least one big hug a day! This date is just to let you and your husband evaluate this important factor in your daughter's life and to give you a good date to just let dad love her with his time, energy, and focus.

To prepare for this date, first make reservations at someplace very upscale, and see to babysitting or alternate plans for any other siblings. This night is for just you, her, and Dad.

After you've got your reservation, there's only one thing to prepare: The Box of Questions. You'll be playing a game at the restaurant using these. First, turn to page 81 and cut the questions into tiny strips. Then, find or make a really special box to place these in.

You might find a little jewelry box and wrap it in festive paper, or you can purchase a little ceramic box that can be your daughter's as a gift at the end of the game. It just needs to be fun and special. (Note: Please read through all of the questions to make sure you are comfortable with them. If for some reason your daughter's father will be replaced by a grandfather, a big brother, or an uncle, please write your own questions using these as guides.)

I want you and your daughter to go all out in dressing up for this date. Why? Well, it seems that even girls who generally dress modestly throw all caution to the wind when they prepare for special occasions. Spaghetti straps, skirts slit up to the thigh, backless gowns, and teenie, tiny mini-dresses defy every SKG Truth or Bare Fashion Test. Take this opportunity to remind your daughter that modesty applies in all settings.

Your SKG Challenge is the dinner date, and at a more elegant restaurant this will take longer than forty-five minutes, so your Girl Gab is rolled into the Challenge in the form of the Box of Questions. In your

Where to Go For Dinner
This is not a night to hit your daughter's favorite Chinese hangout. This is a night to pamper her as she deserves to be pampered.

A Private Bed & Breakfast
Some bed & breakfasts have very quaint settings—that's not what you're looking for—but some have very lavish dining rooms that are available to the public by reservation only. We have one like this in my hometown called The Carnegie House. Bob took me there for our twelfth wedding anniversary. Ooo la la! It sits on a golf course and has a beautiful view. The dining room only holds maybe twenty people or so. It's very exclusive and the prices reflect that. You can check the following Website for ideas: www.bedandbreakfast.com.

A Historical Landmark
The Nittany Lion Inn is a landmark in my hometown. This place has been a gathering for Penn State University hob-nobbing for decades. Every Friday night it has a succulent seafood buffet. Look for landmark restaurants in college towns and historical towns like Williamsburg, Virginia, and San Antonio, Texas. I know those might not be near you, but you get the idea. What is close by?

A Restaurant with a View
My husband and I once dined in the CN Tower, the world's tallest free-standing structure, which is located in Toronto. It was fun to dine high above the city where the restaurant revolved so we could get a view of every direction. There are lots of exciting restaurants with a view. At a place like the American Girl Café (which has locations in Chicago, New York, and Dallas: www.americangirlplace.com), the John Hancock Building in Chicago, or the Space Needle in Seattle, you can make this night one she won't soon forget!

daughter's diary, she'll find a place to record the special things you or her dad said during this time in the restaurant.

OK, check your lipstick and let's go!

SKG • CD • 7-10 Minutes
Play "Date Number Eight: Affirmation of Beauty" from your SKG compact disc as you drive to your destination.

SKG • Challenge • 1 hour 20 minutes +
Get seated and order dinner before you present the SKG Girl Gab Box of Questions. Explain that this is a game you'll be playing. Here's how it works:

1 You'll take turn pulling questions from the box. The person who pulls it tells whom it is for—Dad, Mom, or Daughter—and reads it.

2 The person whom it is for needs to do what is asked of him or her. Most are recalling memories or sharing opinions, so you can't get them right or wrong. But a few are questions to test how well you know each other. If you get this one wrong, you have to put it back to try again if it comes up.

3 The person with the most slips before your entrees arrive gets to select a dessert to share.

SKG • Girl Gab
Your Girl Gab for this date was the Box of Questions, but your daughter has some room in her diary to record key memories. Remind her to take some time to do this either on the way home or when she gets there.

SKG • CD • 3 Minutes
Pop your SKG CD in for the ride home. Christian recording artist Rebecca St. James will share her beauty secrets.

SKG • Driveway Prayer • 5-7 Minutes
Ask your husband to pray over your daughter to complete your date and your SKG experience. His prayer should affirm both her internal and external beauty.

Box of Questions

✂

Dad: God carefully created your daughter with precision and beauty. Describe the first moment you saw your daughter.

Dad: Your daughter has been learning that internal beauty is more important than external beauty. What's the most beautiful thing about her heart?

Dad: Your daughter has been learning than her body has the power to intoxicate guys. Tell her your perspective as a dad on how a guy thinks about girls.

Dad: Beauty is unique features about us that no one else has. What unique feature about your wife attracted you to her?

Mom: How did you tell your daughter's dad you were pregnant with her?

Mom: What part of your daughter's face most looks like you? Her dad?

Mom: What's your daughter's favorite book?

Mom: Fill in the blank. The source of my beauty is *(Answer: the presence of God)*

Daughter: What's the most fun you've ever had with your dad? Why?

Daughter: When do you most sense your dad's love? Is it (a) when he hugs you or (b) when he does things with you? Why?

Daughter: Fill in the blank. My beauty is ultimately determined by what I wear *(Answer: on the inside)*.

Daughter: Tell your dad about the Gestalt Theory. *(Possible Answer: The human brain craves the completion of an incomplete image, so although sometimes we can see only a couple of curvy lines and a dot, our minds create the image of a person.)* How does this relate to fashion?

Daughter: Tell your mom and dad which SKG date was your favorite and why.

Daughter: Name three internal fashions that we should wear. *(Possible Answers: submission, good deeds, a gentle spirit, truth, strength, dignity, etc.)*

SKG Devotions

These devotions are in your daughter's SKG Diary.
They are provided here as an option for you to follow along
and add to your own devotional routine if you'd like.

Week One / Day One

In the Morning I Lay My Requests Before You

"In the morning, O Lord, you hear my voice; in the morning I lay my requests before you and wait in expectation."
PSALM 5:3

I don't know about you, but I'm not much of a morning person. In fact, I can be downright grumpy. But seven years ago God showed me the verse above and others like it. *"In the morning, O LORD, you hear my voice; in the morning, I lay my requests before you and wait in expectation."* Was God really calling ME to get out of bed a few minutes earlier to talk to Him? I confessed to Him that I wasn't sure I could do it and I needed His gentle, loving help.

The most amazing thing happened the very next morning. My alarm went off to get me up to do my devotions and I really, really, really wanted to go back to sleep, but suddenly I heard a tapping at my back door. Who could be tapping at my back door so early? I thought. I dragged myself out of bed, only to find no one there. I crawled back into my warm, comfy bed only to have that tap-tap-tapping rudely call me to check the back door again. I got there and NO ONE was there. I went back into my room and waited, thinking someone must be playing a trick on me.

Soon, the tapping came back. I got down on all fours and snuck out under my dining room table. I was staring at my glass door where I saw the most amazing thing. A tiny bird was sitting on my deck tapping on the glass. HA! What a funny way for God to awaken me, I thought. How tender! How loving! How hilarious! That little bird came back every morning for the next three days, luring me out of bed. (One morning I even had Robby and Lexi sneak out with me to see him so people would actually believe me!) I believe that was God's big answer to me that He really does want my attention first thing in the morning. I confess it has been hard for me, but since that little bird visited my deck I've been giving my best effort to hear God's voice IN THE MORNING!

In Your Journal Today:
Rewrite Psalm 5:3 into your journal and write a prayer to God asking Him to help you to talk to Him "in the morning."

Earnestly I Seek You

READ PSALM 63

"O God, You are my God, earnestly I seek You; my soul thirsts for You."
PSALM 63:1

I have a missionary friend named John who went to a Spanish-speaking country to help build a church. Most of the crew were not Christians, but John wanted to share God's love with them, so he built the church with them. They taught him some Spanish so they could communicate better. One day the missionary supervisor came to see how John was doing. He saw John ask for the hammer and the other guys giggled. He saw John ask for a saw and, again, the guys giggled. The missionary looked concerned. He pulled John to the side and asked him why he was calling the workers bad names when he asked for things. John looked over at the workers, who were howling with laughter. The joke was on John. He didn't know Spanish, and so he didn't know he was actually saying, "Pass the hammer, jerk!" or "Pass the saw, loser!"

Sometimes we have a translation difficulty with the Bible. You see, it wasn't actually written in English. It was written in Hebrew, Greek, and Aramaic. Translating the Bible into English from these very complicated languages was a big task, and so sometimes we get a very simplified version or a version that just doesn't say what God actually meant for us to know. That's why you must study diligently. Today's memory verse is a good example of what I'm talking about. Read the verse at the top of the page.

The word "earnestly" is actually the Hebrew word "scachar," which means "dawn, early, rising in immediate pursuit." In other words, talking to God should be the very first thing we do in the day. If your morning routine is so rushed that you can't spend time with God, try to get up a little earlier. If you're just "not a morning person" it's OK to have your quiet time with God later in the day, but be sure to utter a prayer to give Him your day as you awaken!

In Your Journal Today:

Rewrite Psalm 63:1 into your journal. Write about a day when you really felt "thirsty" for God. What did that feel like? Tell Him!

Seek First the Kingdom of God

READ MATTHEW 6:25–34

"Seek first his kingdom and his righteousness,
and all these things will be given to you as well."
MATTHEW 6:33

When I was not much older than you, I felt like God wanted me to help a ministry teach children about Jesus. I wasn't old enough to actually be a teacher, so I volunteered to be a helper. That same summer a lot of my friends were going to the beach every day and planning a lot of cool things. I felt a little left out, but I kept believing that when I seek God's kingdom first, "all these things" would be given to me as well. For me at that age, "all these things" meant some fun and sun. That summer God blessed me amazingly with a scholarship to the most awesome Christian camp near Pittsburgh. I got to go caving, rock climbing, and horseback riding, and I tried my hand at archery, self-defense, candle-making, and all kinds of stuff. It was so amazing. God really does bless our socks off when we seek His kingdom first.

How do you think that God wants you to seek His kingdom? Is there a friend who isn't the most fun to be with but needs your love right now? Is there someone you need to pray for more?

What are "all these things" in your heart? They're different for all of us. Is it a happier home? Is it a better teacher? Is it more friends? Is it a certain thing you're hoping to do?

Guess what? God already knows about it, and so you might as well tell Him.

In Your Journal Today:

Rewrite Matthew 6:33 into your journal. Write a prayer asking God to show you how you can seek His kingdom and ask Him to help you to do that first rather than trying to get "all these things!" Trust Him to provide them or to change your heart.

Week One /Day Four
Behold I Stand at the Door and Knock
READ REVELATION 3:14–22

"Here I am! I stand at the door and knock. If anyone hears My voice and opens the door, I will come in and eat with him, and he with Me."
REVELATION 3:20

There is a story about a family who was in a flood and prayed for God to rescue them. Soon a boat floated by and a man offered to pick them up. The family said, "No, it's OK, we're waiting for God to rescue us!" After a while longer, a helicopter came by and dropped down a lifeline. The family refused it because they were waiting for God. Hello! Do you think that just maybe God had sent that boat and that helicopter?

Today's verse talks about God standing at the door and knocking. A lot of people use this verse to explain that Jesus is talking to unbelievers and saying He wants to be with them. But that's not an accurate use of this verse. Look at the heading just before verse 14. In my Bible it says, "To the CHURCH in Laodicea!" This verse is written to those who already believe that Jesus is their Savior. And it says, "Here I am! I stand at the door and knock . . . open the door!" Sometimes as believers we really need to slow down and realize that God needs us to respond to something He's already doing in our lives.

Is there something you've been praying about for a while? Is it possible that God has already sent a boat or a helicopter to say "Here I am"? Take a moment today to look around to see where God is knocking at the door of your life.

In Your Journal Today:

Rewrite Revelation 3:20 into your journal. Sit quietly before God today and just let Him reveal to you where maybe He's been knocking at the door of your life. After you do this, write about what God tells you.

———————— ∿∿∾◦◕◵⌖◶◷∾◦∿∿ ————————

Week One /Day Five

Look At Us!
READ ACTS 3:1–10

"Peter looked straight at him, as did John. Then Peter said, 'Look at us!'"
ACTS 3:4

Ever wonder about the term "born again"? In John 3, Jesus tells Nicodemus that he must be "born again." Nicodemus even asks, "How can an old man get back into his mother's belly?" (See verse 4.) But Jesus is talking about something symbolic, not literally being born again. What does it mean?

Well, pretend with me for a moment that you are a baby still stuck in your mother's warm, wet belly. You are fully developed and ready to be born. You can even hear the distant world outside your mother's belly. But what of that world can you see? Nothing, right? No brilliant colors. No sunshine. No rainbows. No smiling faces. No acts of love. You cannot see until you are born. Then suddenly the wonders of this world are fully exposed for you to see.

It's like that for people who don't know Jesus as their Lord and Savior. They just don't "get it" sometimes because they cannot "see" what you see in the spirit world. They can't see God's love. Can't see God's healing. Can't see the warmth of fellowship in a Bible study group. They haven't been born into that world yet.

What can they see? They can see you! Our Bible reading today tells about a man who needed physical healing. It's funny that Peter says, "Look at us!" Why didn't he say, "Look at God"? Two reasons. One, the man wasn't a believer yet, and so he was blind to God. But also because Peter and John were living so very much as God wanted them to, that they could confidently say "Look at us!" knowing that the man would see proof of God. Is your life like that? Can your friends who can't see God see proof of Him in your life?

In Your Journal Today:

Rewrite Acts 3:4 into your journal. In your journal, write a prayer of confession admitting what areas of your life need to better reflect God. Then, ask God to help you to be more like Him in that area so others can see God's power in your life.

———————— ∿∿∾◦◕◵⌖◶◷∾◦∿∿ ————————

Week Two / Day One
Seeing God in His Creation

"I lift up my eyes to the hills—where does my help come from?
My help comes from the Lord, the Maker of heaven and earth."
PSALM 121:1–2

About seven years ago, I was sitting on the beach feeling very sad. I was sitting right where the foam and waves just touch the sand, making it smooth like cement when they subside back into the ocean. I was wondering if God even cared about me because I was so discouraged. So, I asked Him. "God, do You even care?" Suddenly my eye caught some movement on that smooth sand. I moved closer. This time when the waves came up I saw clearly that dozens upon dozens of teenie, tiny clams were being washed onto shore. A few seconds after the water subsided, they all suddenly stood on end like tiny little soldiers and wriggled their way down into the depths of the cool sand. I thought this was amazing that God created these teenie, tiny, insignificant creatures with a way to protect themselves from drying out in the hot sun. Suddenly, it hit me. If God cares about those little clams, of course He cares about me! It was like a big hug from God.

The Bible is full of God communicating to people He loves through His creation.

This week, we're going to look at some ways that God speaks to us through creation . . . and to Y-O-U! You might want to plan to have your devotions outside or near a window you can be close to creation when you are talking to God.

In Your Journal Today:
Rewrite Psalm 121:1–2 into your journal and write a prayer to God asking
Him to help you notice Him in creation this week. Maybe write about a
time when you remember seeing God in creation.

Week Two / Day Two
Burning off the Chaff
READ LUKE 3:15–18

"He will burn up the chaff with unquenchable fire."
LUKE 3:17B

In Australia there are great, horrible "bush" fires. (We might call them forest fires.) When I was visiting Australia, I sat in a restaurant overlooking a valley that had been entirely burned out. The flames had obviously come within feet of the restaurant. I asked my tour guide, "How do they fight the fire?" He replied, "We don't. It's too powerful, and its purpose is really to make the bush stronger, so it must burn." He went on to explain that the trees making up the bush had a cone so hard and so thick that the only thing that would allow the seed to pop out and begin to grow was intense heat. When the cones heated up, they burst and the bush could continue growing. The fire also burned off the weak, dry, and dying trees. So you see, the fire is really a good thing.

John the Baptist said something about fire when the people asked him if He was "the Christ." He said that Jesus would burn up the chaff (the useless, inedible stuff that's left after wheat is harvested—yuck!) with unquenchable fire. In other words, in your life and mine Jesus might sometimes let things get really hard and difficult for us. He does this to burn off the useless things in our lives (the chaff) and to let seeds of growth sprout in us.

Has your family ever been through a hard time? Have you ever wondered why God was allowing it? Wait until you see what God allows to grow in your life before you question what God was up to. It's usually something really good.

In Your Journal Today:

Rewrite Luke 3:17. In your journal, write a prayer to God asking Him to help you to endure the "fire" of something that is really hard for you right now. Tell God that you'll trust Him to make something good grow as He burns away the useless things in your life.

Week Two / Day Three
Even a Donkey
READ NUMBERS 22:21–35

"The donkey saw me and turned away from me these three times. If she had not turned away, I would certainly have killed you by now, but I would have spared her."
NUMBERS 22:33

When was the last time you saw a donkey speak? (Maybe when you watched the movie Shrek, but hey . . . that's only a cartoon!) In the Bible God actually caused a donkey to talk. He used this little creature to both save and direct the man named Balaam. Balaam was going somewhere God didn't want him to go. God was allowing him to go as long as he only said what God wanted him to say. But Balaam struck out on his journey as if he was "the man." God sent an angel to get his attention, but only Balaam's donkey saw him. How many times? Three times! And then, the donkey talked! (Would you have thought you were losing your mind or what?)

My friend, God used a mere donkey. Is He not going to also mightily use you during the course of your life? Oh, He certainly is. Ephesians 4:7 says "He has given each of us a special gift according to the generosity of Christ." [NLT] Jesus has given you a special gift . . . or ability . . . that no one else quite has. (Kind of like giving the gift of speech to a donkey!) He's going to use you in a mighty, magnificent, and powerful way if you will let Him. After all, you are one of His most magnificent creations!

Rewrite Ephesians 4:7 into your journal. Write a prayer asking God to use you and to help you to see the special gift or ability that He has given to you. (It could take a long time to see it. I found my gift when I was twenty-six, but I had a hint about it when I was eight!)

Week Two / Day Four

NOTE: It is best if you do this devotion outside during daylight when you can do some bird watching!

Soar on Wings Like Eagles
READ ISAIAH 40:26–31

"Those who hope in the Lord will renew their strength. They will soar on wings like eagles; they will run and not grow weary, they will walk and not be faint."
ISAIAH 40:31

Today is a good day to have your devotions outside if you can. If you can't, move to a window. I'm praying even now as I write this that the Lord will show you the most beautiful bird today. I'm praying that you'll be able to see one in flight. If you can, go outside and watch and wait for a bird to fly above you. Just sit quietly and think about God as you watch birds nearby. Imagine that this is the freedom with which God wants you to live every day. Let God speak to you.

Week Two / Day Five
The Circle of the Earth
READ ISAIAH 40:21–22

"He sits enthroned above the circle of the earth."
ISAIAH 40:22

How do you know that this Bible you're reading is real and true and written by God? Think about it for a minute. It's a hard question to answer, isn't it? Oh my sweet friend, all of your life you will be searching for more and more proof that this Bible is real. And today I want to show you a secret treasure in the Bible that helps us to know that it is.

Read Isaiah 40:22 again. Where does it say that God sits? Above the circle of the earth, right? Wait a minute! This book was written when people still believed the earth was FLAT! How on earth did the writer know that the earth was a circle? (It would be years before anyone guessed that the earth was round, and when they did, people tried to kill them because it was so unbelievable to them!) This Bible verse can only be explained by one thing. The God of the universe who created the earth and knew it was a circle must have inspired the writer to say such a thing.

Astronaut John Glenn is a Christian. He says that he knew the moment he believed that Jesus was the Christ. It was when he was in outer space looking through a tiny window in his spacecraft back to the round, quiet earth. He thought of this Bible verse and suddenly realized, "God had to have inspired that truth!"

You can be certain that God is and that what He has inspired in the Bible is true to the highest degree.

In Your Journal Today:

Rewrite Isaiah 40:22 into your journal. In your journal,
write a prayer of praise to God that is three sentences long. Use only things
about creation to praise Him. Be creative!

Week Three / *Day One*
Praise God with Your Tongue!

"Whoever would love life and see good days must keep his tongue from evil and
his lips from deceitful speech."
1 PETER 3:10

OK, you may have already figured this out, but you're a girl! (What a concept!) As a girl you tend to talk a whole lot more than you would if you were a guy. Seriously, people have studied this. In one study, they watched pre-schoolers play. The boys? They were making all kinds of gross and loud noises. You can only imagine! The girls? Well, they were conversing as if they could fix all the problems in the world! In a study of adults they found that the average man speaks something like 10,000 words a day. Now that is a lot, but a woman speaks almost three times that many words. Talking is good, but God's Word tells us again and again that talking is something we have to be very careful with. So, we're going to spend all week talking to God about talking.

For today, I want you to praise God for the gift of speech. (Isn't it interesting that we praise God with talking?!) Go ahead! I want you to write a nice loooooong letter of praise to God. Just so you have an example, here's my praise about speech.

"Oh God, I thank You that You've given me the ability to speak. I praise You that I can tell my kids that I love them. I praise You that I can sing songs of worship. I'm thankful that I can giggle and tell jokes. God, let my lips always be a blessing to You!"

In Your Journal Today:

Rewrite 1 Peter 3:10 into your journal and write your praise to
God for your ability to speak.

Taming the Tongue
READ JAMES 3:3–6

*"When we put bits into the mouths of horses to make them obey us,
we can turn the whole animal."*
JAMES 3:3

Once I was riding horseback with my friend in Missouri. It was all going along very nicely until we turned around to head home. The crazy animal couldn't wait to get there, I guess. It took off at lightning speed, and I was scared silly. I thought surely I would fall off, and so I tried to slow that beast with the bridle and reins. But nothing worked. Eventually I just held on and enjoyed the ride! I couldn't control the animal.

The Bible tells us that sometimes our tongues are like that. Uncontrollable. Girls sometimes struggle with this. I heard about two girls who showed up at youth group one night with almost the exact same new haircut. One girl squinted her eyes and said, "She's always trying to copy me. She did this on purpose." How silly. (And stupid.) But it was just enough to make the second girl feel really bad and use a few cruel words of her own.

Have you ever had a friend say cruel things to you? Do you remember how it made you feel? It hurts, doesn't it?

God wants you to control your mouth just like a bit controls a horse. Do you need to work on this area of your life?

In Your Journal Today:
*Rewrite James 3:3 and then confess to God a time that your tongue
was out of control and you said something unkind to someone.
Ask God to forgive you and to help you be kind.*

Lying and Dying
Read Psalm 119:33-40

"Truthful lips endure forever, but a lying tongue lasts only a moment."
PROVERBS 12:19

A few months ago I was asking God to show me if there were any lies in my life. I felt God telling me that I needed to be free of lying, but I just couldn't think why He was talking to me about this. I prayed that He would show me. The next day my mom brought out a beautiful clay pot that I had made in seventh grade. Only . . . I didn't make it. I always felt so good when I'd bring home a really neat art project and she praised it, so one day I brought home a piece of art that I did not make. Not only did I steal it, but I had lived with the lie of it for years. Soon I was confessing it to my mom and being set free from a lie told long ago.

Ya know, God doesn't like lying much. I think that's why old Ananias and Sapphira fell down dead . . . because they lied. Sometimes a lie can be big and bad like the one I told about the pot. Or sometimes it can be an exaggeration such as "I was on my best behavior in lunch today" when you really were a part of the group that got in trouble. Or a lie can be failing to speak up in truth, like when a teacher asks who did something bad in class and you just don't say anything even though you know. God doesn't mess with lying. He hates it.

But He loves truth. Is there an area in your life where you need to work on being more truthful?

In Your Journal Today:

Rewrite Proverbs 12:19 and then write to God about a time that you were not truthful. If it involves your parents, please go to them and confess it to them also.

Week Three / *Day Four*

To Give Courage

READ 2 CORINTHIANS 7:13–14

Today's devotion is just a touch . . . a peek . . . into the apostle Paul's pride for his friends in Corinth. See how he uses words like "encourage" and "boasted" and "delighted"!

One day when I was a little down, Lexi snuck off and bought a special card and wrote me a note of encouragement. It changed my whole week!

God wants you to be an encourager. (Encourage means "to give courage.") For devotions today, I want you to write a nice note to a friend encouraging her for being a good Christian. Or, if the friend you're writing to isn't a Christian, thank her for being a good friend. Be specific about what you're thanking her for—what do you like about her?

In Your Journal Today:

No journal writing. Write a note and give it to a friend.

Week Three / *Day Five*

Confession

"Confess your sins to each other and pray for each other so that you may be healed."
JAMES 5:16

Sin makes us sick. Some kinds of sin make us physically sick, but all kinds of sin make us emotionally sick. Can you remember ever feeling really bad about something you did wrong? Well, today I want to share with you God's prescription for that sickness. James 5:16 tells us that when we confess our sins to each other, we are healed. Now don't be confused. Only God can forgive your sins, and don't let anyone tell you otherwise. You can confess your sins to God, and you must to be forgiven. But He has given us each other here on earth to help with the hurt. So, the healing for the sickness that sin causes comes from telling someone. (And that someone can help you not to do the same thing again.)

Secrets aren't a good thing when it comes to sin. I remember keeping a secret from my mom for years about a bad thing I did. I was so ashamed. I felt lonely and sad about it. Then, one day I managed to tell her about it and suddenly I felt great. My mom wasn't super mad like I thought she'd be. She was a little disappointed, but she helped me to figure out why I sinned like this and to make decisions so that I would not do it again. Don't let another day go by without telling your mom about anything you've done that needs to be confessed. You'll be glad you did.

In Your Journal Today:

Rewrite James 5:16. Today, write in your journal about something you need your mom's help with. Is it talking more kindly to your friends? Is it being more truthful? Confess this to her after you write about it, and watch to see how God will make your heart feel much better!

Week Four / *Day One*

Looking at the Heart
READ 1 SAMUEL 16:2–13

"Man looks at the outward appearance, but the Lord looks at the heart."
1 SAMUEL 16:7B

A homeless man in a tiny little town was accused of stealing a large basket of goods from a little grocery store. The police showed up at the grocery store with the homeless man and the stolen goods. The grocer showed much compassion. Rather than pressing charges for theft, he simply said, "Oh, I'm glad they brought you back! You left so quickly that you forgot your change." And he pulled out $38.12 and gave it to the homeless man and sent him on his way with the basket of goods.

Just a few days later the grocer was called to a lawyer's office. The lawyer explained that the homeless man had died and had willed all his earthly goods to the grocer. The lawyer handed the grocer a dingy, dirty bag. In that bag was some old bread, a Bible, and a bank book. The last deposit in the book was for $38.12, which brought the balance to just over $3 million.

The grocer's kindness was rewarded greatly, don't you think? The grocer did not look at the man's outward appearance, but he looked at his heart and his needs. And he showed much kindness.

In our Bible reading today, you see that God did the same thing when He selected David to be king of Israel. When Samuel went to find the future king, he was at first sure God must be talking about Jesse's oldest, strongest, wisest son. But He wasn't. He was sending Samuel to select David, who was Jesse's youngest, smallest son, and who still had much to learn.

Be kind to people. You may only see how they look today, but God sees their future and you might be an important part of it.

Rewrite 1 Samuel 16:7b. Write a letter to God about a person in your life who needs kindness but whose appearance is difficult for you to get past.

Week Four / *Day Two*

A Wall of Faith
READ EPHESIANS 6:10–17

"Take up the shield of faith, with which you can extinguish all the flaming arrows of the evil one."
EPHESIANS 6:16

In Bible days, there were a lot of terrible wars and battles. Each warrior had a shield to deflect the enemy's attack. The shield was thick and powerful and carefully crafted with ridges on the sides. When the attack was particularly difficult, the warriors would lock their shields together using the ridges and grooves to link them like puzzle pieces. They would then have an entire wall built in front of them to keep the enemy away.

Ephesians tells us that we need to have a shield of faith to protect ourselves from our enemy, Satan. It seems to me that, since the warriors linked themselves together with their shields, God used this analogy not only to tell us to be prepared to deflect the enemy's attack but to tell us to be prepared with friends and family members whose faith we can link into when the battle is heavy.

Which friends, family members, teachers, and church leaders do you spend time with? Are they believers whose faith is strong? If you were having a hard time, could you lock your shield of faith into theirs?

In Your Journal Today:
Rewrite Ephesians 6:16 into your journal. Write the names of people who came to mind as you read today's devotion . . . people around you whose faith is strong. Thank God for them.

Week Four / *Day Three*

Too Much TV?
PSALM 119:33–37

"Turn my eyes away from worthless things; preserve my life according to your word."
PSALM 119:37

My dad was the first kid on his block to have a television. (Think about it! I bet a lot of your grandparents never saw TV until they were your age! Strange, huh?) When I was your age, my dad had already logged a good twenty years on the tube, but one day he pulled quite a trick on me. He sat in his TV viewing chair and said, "Watch this! Today I learned how to magically change the TV channel." Then, he'd wave his fingers in the air and the channel would change. I was amazed. He did this again and again—turning the TV on and off and changing channels with a flick of his fingers. The joke was on me. I was the first kid on the block to have a remote control!

Today, the average kid your age watches three hours of television a day. (That's a lot of TV!) If they keep up at that rate, they'll see nearly eight thousand murders. Do you think that will affect them?

There are a lot of things in our world that can be considered "worthless things," and many of today's TV shows are among them. It can be hard to change your viewing habits if you're watching too much or the wrong kinds of things. You might try not watching any TV for a week. Or set a goal of only thirty minutes a day.

How are you doing? Are you filling your mind with worthless things, or are you allowing God to preserve your life with His Word?

In Your Journal Today:
Rewrite Psalm 119:37 and ask God to help you to monitor your television viewing habits.

Week Four / Day Four
A Father's Love
READ LUKE 15:11–24

"For God so loved the world that He gave His only begotten son, that whoever believes in Him will not perish but have everlasting life."
JOHN 3:16 (KJV)

There was a young man who'd grown up on an almond farm in California. He didn't want to be a farmer, so he asked his wealthy father for some money and left home. He left with a bad attitude. He found himself adventure in the form of a lot of sin. Eventually he realized how awful his life had become and how very much he missed his father. But he had become so worn out and broken. Of what use was he to his family now?

He sent his father a note. It said, "Father, I've sinned, and I want to come home. At 1:00 tomorrow I'll be on the train to come home, and it goes right past one corner of your tree orchard. Please cover one tree with a white sheet if I am welcomed. If I don't see it, I'll just stay on the train. Your humble son."

The next day, as the train neared the property, the son began to weep. He was so distraught he couldn't get himself to look. So, he asked an old man sitting nearby, "Sir, in a moment we're going to round a bend and you'll see the most beautiful orchard imaginable. Could you please look to see if one of those trees is covered in a white sheet?" The kind old man agreed to look. In a few moments the old man said, "Son, I think you need to see this for yourself." As far as the eye could see, every tree was covered with a sheet.

That's how very much God our Father loves you, my friend. There is

NOTHING you can ever do to make Him love you less. While He does not desire for you to know the pain of living a life without Him and filled with sin, He's always ready to welcome you back.

In Your Journal Today:

Is there any area of your life that you need to give back to Him? A friendship? Your relationship with your parents? Bad music or too much TV? Write about that today in your journal.

Week Four / *Day Five*
You Are Beautiful
READ 1 PETER 3:3–4

"Your beauty . . . should be that of your inner self, the unfading beauty of a gentle and quiet spirit, which is of great worth in God's sight."
1 PETER 3:3–4

You are beautiful, my precious SKG! You are so fantastically lovely in your own unique way. Remember how all of this began with 1 Peter 3:3–4. Some people use verse 3, which says, "Your beauty should not come from outward adornment, such as braided hair and the wearing of gold jewelry and fine clothes" to say that we can't dress beautifully. But . . . the original Greek language really said simply "clothes" and not "fine clothes." (Maybe your version says that.) Anyway, the point is that we'd all be running around naked if we took this to mean God did not want us to braid our hair or wear nice clothes and jewelry. It doesn't mean anything without verse 4. What God is really saying is this: "Are you spending more time with Me . . . making your heart beautiful . . . than you are spending on making your body beautiful?" He loves you, and He knows that spending time alone with Him gives you confidence, helps you to know your value in Christ, steers you in the right direction, and gives you internal beauty.

This is our last devotion for SKG, but I hope it won't be your last devotion. There are still lots of pages to fill up in that journal of yours. Fill it, my precious friend. Fill it and see how much more beautiful you become.

In Your Journal Today:

Rewrite 1 Peter 3:4. Today I want you to write a letter to your dad or mom telling him or her how having devotions has been helpful for you. Ask your parents if they can help you purchase something that will help you to keep having devotions.
